Outstanding teaching in lifelong learning

This boo~

Outstanding teaching in lifelong learning

Harriet Harper

Open University Press

Open University Press
McGraw-Hill Education
McGraw-Hill House
Shoppenhangers Road
Maidenhead
Berkshire
England
SL6 2QL

email: enquiries@openup.co.uk
world wide web: www.openup.co.uk

and Two Penn Plaza, New York, NY 10121-2289, USA

First published 2013

A catalogue record of this book is available from the British Library

ISBN-13: 978-0-335-26262-5
ISBN-10: 0-335-26262-7
eISBN: 978-0-335-26263-2

Library of Congress Cataloging-in-Publication Data
CIP data applied for

Typeset by Aptara, Inc.

Fictitious names of companies, products, people, characters and/or data that may be
used herein (in case studies or in examples) are not intended to represent any real
individual, company, product or event.

Printed and bound by CPI Group (UK) Ltd, Croydon, CR0 4YY

To Naomi and Alex

Praise for this book

"At the heart of *Outstanding Teaching* are twenty lessons judged by inspectors to be outstanding. Each group of four is considered under the heading of a key theme related to outstanding teaching, such as 'prudent planning' and 'passion and enthusiasm', preceded by a perceptive analysis of that theme and then each lesson is described and clearly analysed in terms of what made it outstanding. There is a consistent and intelligent use of theory to illuminate the practice analysed. For the first time, in my view, the gap between inspection, practice and teacher education in the Lifelong Learning sector has been superbly bridged and Harriet Harper, as an experienced teacher educator and HMI, could not be in a better position to do this. At the end of the book, she brings together commonalities of the outstanding lessons and compellingly debunks ten myths surrounding practice, observation and inspection. Although *Outstanding Teaching* should be compulsory reading for all those managing, teaching or training to teach in the sector, those from other phases, primary, secondary and HE, will find the book enormously helpful because the key knowledge, skills and understanding that lead to outstanding teaching are so eminently transferable across phases."

Andy Armitage is Head of the Department of Post-Compulsory Education at Canterbury Christ Church University. In 2011–12, he was seconded to Ofsted to inspect initial teacher education for the Lifelong Learning sector.

"*Outstanding Teaching in Lifelong Learning* is an accessible, research-informed, empirical study. It takes the complexities of teaching and the role of teachers' professional judgment in different and unfolding contexts seriously. It brings together empirical and academic research from a range of disciplines, including the arts, humanities, science and vocational specialisms, to provide useful insights into what good teachers do and don't do.

Like many other concepts in education 'outstanding teaching' is widely used and frequently misunderstood. Although it is relatively easy to identify teaching which stands out because it is particularly 'good' it can be much more difficult to pin down what it is that makes it so. This can lead us to abandon our efforts.

On the other hand the outcomes of those who have attempted to conduct research into 'outstanding' teaching have ranged from the production of 'recipes' or 'tips for teachers', to checklists, which claim to identify 'ideal' (often idealised) types or characteristics of the 'perfect' teacher most of us would cross the street to avoid!

Outstanding Teaching in Lifelong Learning is not a handbook for those who seek a comprehensive and neat distillation of 'outstanding' teaching. Instead, it offers credible, realistic and perceptive glimpses into the classroom practices of teachers who care about education and the educational values which shape their practice.

This book will be of interest to experienced and intending teachers, teacher educators, and education mangers across the lifelong learning sector, as well as those working in schools and higher education settings."

Dr Maggie Gregson is Reader in Education at the University of Sunderland and also Director of the Centre for Excellence in Teacher Training (SUNCETT)

"Freedom to teach...this book provides an outstanding contribution to debates about the importance of teaching and teachers. It offers teachers, across all sectors, credible examples of what makes an outstanding lesson and adds an accessible, intellectual framework to discussions which seem to have disappeared amongst practitioners, inspectorates and policy makers."

Ela Piotrowska is Principal of Morley College

Contents

Lessons

Acknowledgements

Thanks to colleagues I have worked with, teachers whose lessons I have observed and all the students and teacher trainees I have taught over several decades in both further and higher education, from whom I have learned so much. I am particularly indebted to the following people who provided examples of outstanding practice: Lynda Cole, Gloria Dolan, Alex Falconer, Nigel Flood, Pippa Francis, Alan Hinchliffe, Anne Keelan-Towner, Alan Marsh, Tony Noonan, Sandra Tweedie and Kathy Tyler. I am very grateful to Andrew Armitage for reading a draft version of the book and providing feedback. Thanks also to Andreas Credé.

1 Introduction

What is the book about?

This book is about teaching and teachers. The decision to avoid the much used phrase 'learning and teaching' in the book title is deliberate. For many years now, as noted by Coffield (2008: 7), teachers, managers and researchers in the educational world have been focusing almost exclusively on the word 'learning' in a well-intentioned and understandable attempt to remind everyone about the importance of students. However, in doing so, they have downplayed the significance of teachers. Through the examination of lessons judged to be outstanding, this book explores the practice of highly skilled teachers.

Who is the book for?

The 20 real lessons that form the basis for the book all took place within what is known as the lifelong learning sector. For this reason, the content will be of most interest to those who intend to teach in the same sector or to those who already work in it. Most of the issues discussed are also applicable to schools and higher education and so will be relevant for trainees, teachers and teacher educators in these sectors, too.

Even those who work in the incredibly diverse lifelong learning sector often struggle to define it and find the easiest way is to state what the sector is not rather than try to list its many components. In effect, it is everything outside schools and higher education institutions. However, as the boundaries between sectors are becoming more blurred, even this definition is not quite correct. The sector is known by some as being the local further education (FE) college, where young people acquire skills for a particular job. For others, it is where students can take or retake a wide range of courses, because they did not get high enough grades at school or because they want a more 'grown up' environment. FE colleges have long been a refuge for those who have failed in other educational institutions and the sector is rich in examples of triumph over adversity. In some cases, though, it means tough competition to get into the local sixth-form college that specializes in A level programmes. Increasingly, for some it is an alternative to university for higher education courses. For adults, it is a place in which they can undertake courses and gain qualifications to increase the likelihood of finding employment, to change their career or improve their basic skills. Few, except those who work in this particular part of the sector, associate it with prison or young offender education. Many more think about it in terms of part-time day or evening recreational courses in adult and community learning centres, while others focus on employers and the growth of apprenticeships and work-based learning providers.

In summarizing the lifelong learning sector, Lingfield (2012: 1) suggests it is:

> varied in purpose; very large in terms of overall size; ranging across public, private and charitable organisations from the small and specialised to, increasingly, big educational businesses with national and international reach; and dependent for its quality on the creativity, confidence and sense of professional self-worth of nearly 200,000 teaching staff.

With such diversity, a lack of clarity as to its aim has always been an issue for the sector. In noting this, Lingfield (2012: 2) helpfully categorizes the sector into five main segments:

- remedial FE, redressing the shortcomings of schooling
- community FE, offering lifelong learning opportunities to local people, with benefits to their health, longevity and well-being, as well as continuing education
- vocational FE, teaching occupational skills
- academic courses
- higher education studies.

The lessons that form the basis for this book reflect the first four in this list. They include disciplines in the arts and humanities, literacy and numeracy, and laboratory science subjects as well as vocational specialisms such as animal care, hospitality and motor vehicle studies. The implications of having these distinct segments on making judgements about teaching are discussed in Chapter 7.

What does outstanding mean?

This book is about outstanding teaching. The adjective 'outstanding' is preferable to 'excellent' or 'exceptional' in the context of this book for two reasons. Firstly, it is used in its literal sense in that these lessons stand out among others of their kind. Secondly, the lessons described were observed by Her Majesty's Inspectors (HMI) and judged to be a 'grade 1', the descriptor for which is 'outstanding'.

This justification for the book title should not be used to mask the fact that any definition of outstanding teaching is inherently problematic. What constitutes good, effective, excellent or outstanding teaching continues to be the subject of national and international research and debate across all phases of education. It depends on who defines the concept, why they do so, what criteria they use and how they judge it. In this respect, it is usually highly contentious and political. In the school and lifelong learning sectors, the term outstanding has been hijacked by Ofsted and has unfortunately – and often undeservedly – come to be associated with a particular type of success within a narrow, instrumentalist 'checklist' approach to teaching, rather than an exciting and intellectually challenging activity.

Instead of attempting to define the term 'outstanding' and then looking for examples to illuminate and support the suggested definition, this book has as its starting point detailed information about 20 real lessons, with an emphasis on what actually happened in the classroom, workshop or workplace. From these lessons, attempts are made to extrapolate the features they have in common.

Given the small sample, the diversity of the sector and the complex nature of teaching and learning, the intention is not to provide a 'recipe book' for practitioners or managers. Neither is it the intention to promote the primacy of the views of HMI or of one teaching method over another. While the lessons may provoke reflection and provide ideas, it is not possible to take the practice described in these lessons and simply transfer it to other settings. Every single lesson is different and contingent on the professional judgement of the teacher in that particular setting, at that time and with that particular group of students. For this reason, the term 'best practice' is avoided in this book on the basis that it implies there is only one single transferable teaching and learning method that can be applied to all lessons. What works well in one context may not in another and the transfer of good practice, assuming one can agree on what that is, is both complex and time intensive (Eraut 2004).

Numerous attempts have been made by various government bodies and quality improvement agencies, particularly over the last 20 years or so, to identify and define 'excellence' so that it can be disseminated, with a view to raising standards across the sector. However, these interpretations of excellence, or good practice, as critically examined by Coffield and Edward (2009), have not led to shared understanding within the sector. It remains the case that political imperatives, inspection and assessment drive the teaching and learning agenda, rather than discussions about **pedagogy**.

Many in the sector would agree with the view that there is not a strong culture of using pedagogical research to inform teaching practice. As noted in research by the Tavistock Institute (2002), the communities that do discuss pedagogy in the lifelong learning sector are quite closed and self-referencing and the important questions about what actually works and how this should be measured remain largely unanswered. The purpose of this book is to look at teaching practice at the micro-level in lessons that have been judged by professionals in this community to be exceptionally good, to identify common or typical features and to examine the extent to which the teaching approaches align to any particular learning theories. This will not determine whether or not what is being measured is 'correct', neither will it provide a definitive description of outstanding teaching. However, it will go some way to establishing and making explicit what one section within this community perceives to be outstanding practice.

Methodology

The author asked HMI and former HMI who specialize in the lifelong learning sector the following question:

> *Of all the lessons you have observed and graded over the years, which ones stood out as truly excellent?*

Interestingly, responses to this question highlight the fact that HMI remember very few lessons, despite observing and grading several thousand between them over many years. 'They all blur into one' was a common refrain. The ones they did recall, though, stood out in their memory because they were either absolutely disastrous or exceptionally good. As intriguing as the former group might be, it is the latter that informs this book. Because of the high volume of observations they undertake and the passing of time, HMI did not remember in which institutions these particular lessons took place or the dates, although at the time the lessons would have featured in and/or contributed to the relevant inspection or good practice reports, all of which are in the public domain.

Readers will be quick to point out the potential problems associated with this methodologically fraught approach. These will include questions about interpretations of excellence, subjectivity and inconsistencies among different HMI, as well the extent to which the notion of 'outstanding' changes over time. Perhaps the main concern will be the suggestion that it is not possible to make judgements about the quality of teaching based solely on the observation of one lesson, particularly during an inspection, when teachers know they will be observed. These issues will be explored in turn.

Lesson observations, although well established now as a familiar part of the quality assurance landscape, remain a source of anxiety for many teachers and managers. Research in the lifelong learning sector (O'Leary 2012) suggests that some teachers adapt their teaching to what they or their managers believe to be the preferred model of a good or outstanding lesson, sometimes even with pressure to present a rehearsed lesson in the presence of an external observer. The observation of teaching and learning has an important part to play in the continuing professional development of teachers. O'Leary (2012) agrees, but argues for a move away from 'restrictive' practice, with its emphasis on observation as a performative tool, to an 'expansive' approach, focusing on the process as a way to gather evidence about teaching and learning, provide useful feedback and promote good practice.

Whether the purpose is to measure effectiveness or to contribute to continuing professional development, it is impossible to avoid subjectivity when observing a lesson. This applies as much to teacher educators and external examiners observing their trainees and college managers making judgements about new or experienced teachers, as it does to HMI. Clear guidelines, explicit criteria, grade descriptor exemplars, joint observations and moderation are all useful in minimizing inconsistency, but the quality of teaching is inherently difficult to measure. The author and the HMI involved in this project, although very experienced, are not exempt from such subjectivity.

Research into the extent to which conceptions of teaching excellence change over time is scarce in relation to the lifelong learning sector, due in part to its complexity, regular changes in policy direction and to the fact that it appears to lack the coherence of the school and higher education sectors. This is reflected in confusion as to the label it is given. It is also known as the 'learning and skills' or 'post-compulsory' sector or simply 'further education'. Over the last 20 years, few would argue, though, with the view that there has been a move, especially in the UK, USA and Europe, towards more 'student-centred', informal and interactive teaching in all educational sectors, with far less emphasis on the transmission of authoritative knowledge by the teacher to passive and compliant students.

Fashions, fads, government initiatives and technological innovations come and go, with varying degrees of impact and success on teaching in the lifelong learning sector. Lesson plan templates have expanded over the years, requiring teachers to comment on all sorts of 'additional' factors and these will be explored in the next chapter. In this context, it is understandable that it can be difficult at times to maintain focus on the 'core business' of teaching which, in effect, has not changed to any great degree. It remains a teacher's role to plan, teach and assess.

The focus in this book is unashamedly on what happens in a lesson. Of course, one has to take into account the fact that, knowing they might be observed, teachers will understandably have taken extra care to prepare their lessons and that during the lesson the teacher and students may behave differently because a stranger is present. The extent to which teachers can put on a performance and 'deliver' a one-off excellent lesson is discussed in one of the myths in Chapter 8. It is not within the remit of this book to address the wider longitudinal issues associated with making judgements about the quality of teaching across the sector or in a particular institution or context. This would involve analysis of the curriculum on offer, students' outcomes and progress, leadership and management and continuing professional development for staff, among many other factors.

The fact that the book focuses on observation of practice does not detract from a recognition that students learn outside the classroom, laboratory or workshop and that many activities underpin and contribute to a teacher's 'performance' in a lesson. In defining 'pedagogy', Alexander (2008: 29) suggests it is:

> the observable act of teaching together with its attendant discourse of educational theories, values, evidence and justifications. It is what one needs to know, and the skills one needs to command, in order to make and justify the many different kinds of decisions of which teaching is constituted.

This definition involves two elements, one dealing with the 'observable act' of teaching, and the other with the knowledge, values, beliefs and justifications that inform it. This book focuses on those observable acts but the second element, which underpins the outstanding lessons, comes through loud and clear.

Educational theories

The teachers of these outstanding lessons, like all teachers, hold their own educational theories, consciously or subconsciously, and these shape the way they teach and the assumptions they make about how their students learn. They influence their teaching style, their choice of material and the way in which they present it. This also applies to HMI, teacher educators, managers and external examiners, who similarly observe lessons through the lens of their own theoretical perspective.

To gain insights into aspects of practice in these outstanding lessons, references are made in the book to different theories and approaches to teaching and learning as well as to specific educationalists or psychologists. This is helpful in that it sets the outstanding lessons in the context of the work of those individuals who have undertaken considerable research, thought deeply about teaching and learning and written extensively on the subject. The book draws not just on literature relating to the lifelong learning sector, but also on research into teaching and learning in schools and in higher education.

Inevitably, the literature choice is personal and selective and reflects studies or individuals the author considers to be of particular interest and relevance. The 'pick and mix' approach to theories or individuals may appear to be somewhat eclectic and, in the next five chapters, it is based more on reference to tools for practice than on ideology. In Chapter 7, though, these are drawn together to look in a more coherent way at the extent to which they fit into one or more teaching and learning approaches.

Definitions and terminology

Reference is made in the book where appropriate to 'teaching and learning' as a singular, rather than plural, noun. This is because the author's definition of teaching encompasses learning. If teaching does not lead to someone learning, then it is not teaching. Instead, it may simply be something akin to talking, listening, demonstrating, observing or testing. Learning, by the same token, can be – and often is – independent of teaching, as people learn in all sorts of ways and in a wide range of different contexts, both within and outside a formal educational environment.

The term 'pedagogy' has already been mentioned and defined. As discussed, it is commonly used to refer to the approaches and underpinning values associated with teaching in the higher education and lifelong learning sectors, as well as in schools. Adult educators, though, often prefer to cite **andragogy** when discussing the practice of teaching adults. The assumptions made by the terms 'pedagogy' and 'andragogy' in relation to teaching and also how people learn will be examined more fully in Chapter 5. Research by the Tavistock Institute (2002: 11) concludes that it remains unclear as to whether fundamental understanding about how people learn has changed in any absolute sense or whether people have just become more adept at making connections between pedagogy and practice.

In common parlance, 'learning' is taken to mean the process by which people acquire new knowledge, skills and understanding, but there is no agreed definition of learning among experts in this field. A **behaviourist** will argue that learning is about a change in behaviour while a **constructivist** would suggest that learning is about seeing the meaning or significance of an experience or concept. A **cognitivist** definition would focus on the way in which students gain and organize their knowledge. Many definitions, though, attempt to combine this cognitive psychological interpretation with a sociocultural perspective, which examines how knowledge, skills and attitudes are constructed.

Judgements about the extent to which students 'learn' in the lessons reviewed in this book are dependent on context and the measurement of this effectiveness is itself context dependent. How learning is viewed in the lifelong learning sector depends, to a large degree, on a more fundamental question about the purpose of this sector. Perceptions might be of a sector that is solely about gaining employability skills and is obsessed with qualifications, in which case learning is primarily instrumental and pragmatic. If, by way of contrast, the view is of a sector that is emancipatory and transforms the lives of young people and adults, then the interpretation of learning is likely to be much broader. In effect, the lifelong learning sector manages in its own inimitable way to accommodate aspects of both perspectives.

The two definitions of learning below both focus more on the latter perception but could incorporate elements of the former:

> Learning...that reflective activity which enables the learner to draw upon previous experience to understand and evaluate the present, so as to shape future action and formulate new knowledge
> (Abbott 1994 in Research Matters 2002: 1)

> Learning refers only to significant changes in capability, understanding, knowledge, practices, attitudes or values by individuals, groups, organisations or society. Two qualifications. It excludes the acquisition of factual information when it does not contribute to such changes; it also excludes immoral learning as when prisoners learn from other inmates in custody how to extend their repertoire of criminal activities.
> (Coffield 2008: 7)

These definitions, both of which exclude the idea of passive knowledge acquisition and measurable outcomes, will be revisited as the lessons in this book are reviewed in the next five chapters. The first definition is useful in that it emphasizes an active process focusing on the accommodation and assimilation of new ideas and experiences. However, with the observation of a single lesson, it is easier to ascertain links between students' past and present learning than it is to recognize any impact on their future. The second definition may be problematic in terms of defining what constitutes 'significant' changes in a given lesson, but it is helpful in specifying that the changes may occur not just in capability and practice, but also in attitude and values. Both definitions are applicable to learning in lessons that are vocational, academic, community or remedial.

Labels given to students, teachers and courses in the lifelong learning sector, in the context of debates about the nature of vocationalism and the academic versus vocational divide, are not value free. For pragmatic reasons, the terminology in this book follows common practice in the sector. The word 'vocational' is used to describe those lessons that would clearly come under the label of 'vocational' in the sector. 'Student', rather than 'learner', is used except where all the participants in a lesson are adults or apprentices. In these cases, the terms 'adult learner' and 'apprentice' are used.

Structure of the book

The lessons are all different and include a wide range of subject areas but they have a number of pedagogical features in common. These characteristics are reflected in five themes, with a chapter devoted to each. The reader is introduced to these lessons gradually, with four in each of the next five chapters, although in effect any of the lessons could be used to illustrate any of the themes. While lesson descriptions aim to capture the flavour and key activities of each lesson as accurately and vividly as possible, it should be noted that the information is based wholly on recollection and so inevitably may be subject to some degree of inadvertent memory distortion. Therefore, some facts, for example about the gender split, the precise number of students in the lesson and the timings, may not always be correct. Each lesson description is followed by a commentary.

Chapter 2 addresses planning. Excellent planning was a feature of all the outstanding lessons and this chapter serves to reinforce the fact that there is much more to teaching than simply what happens during the lesson and that, as discussed above, teachers' planning is informed by their assumptions, values and beliefs. This chapter focuses on the planning of teaching approaches, assessment methods and the use of resources. In doing so, the significance of **learning outcomes** is discussed. The four lessons are numeracy, human anatomy and physiology, skills for life, and geography.

Chapter 3 is about teachers' passion and enthusiasm, both of which came across strongly in all 20 lessons. The chapter also highlights the significance of teachers' subject expertise and the extent to which their teaching skills are both generic and rooted in their discipline. The fact that many of the teachers are 'dual professionals', or 'teacher-practitioners', plays a key role in their ability to share their expertise and enthusiasm with their students. The four lessons are hospitality, classical civilization, art and design, and physics.

Chapter 4 is dedicated to the very skilful way in which the teachers used questioning. Although many other assessment methods were also employed, questioning featured in all the lessons and this aspect of teachers' practice was particularly impressive. The expertise with which teachers elicited responses, challenged students, checked the level of their under-standing and maintained momentum through questions was central to the success of these lessons. The four lessons are statistics, motor vehicle studies, English for speakers of other languages (ESOL), and animal care.

Chapter 5 focuses on high expectations. In different ways, teachers of the outstanding lessons all demanded high standards of work and their students responded readily to this approach. The extent to which students' motivation was a product of this excellent teaching, as opposed to a prereq-uisite, is discussed. The subtle and highly effective classroom management techniques used by the teachers are also examined. The four lessons are media studies, social work, hairdressing, and cleaning and support services.

Chapter 6 is about **inclusive practice**. Dimensions of diversity are introduced and teachers' practice is reviewed in two stages to highlight the ways in which inclusive values and practice permeated the lessons. This involves, firstly, examining what the teachers did in terms of preparation and then, secondly, what happened during the lessons to make then 'inclu-sive'. The four lessons are information technology, bricklaying, teacher education, and family learning.

Chapter 7 addresses overarching questions, such as the extent to which there is a typical kind of outstanding lesson, in terms of subject, setting, student age group or type of teacher. Reflecting on the 20 lessons, the most common teaching and assessment methods are identified and discussed, before looking at where these lessons fit best in terms of educational theo-ries or approaches to teaching.

Chapter 8 identifies and dispels some of the myths about observation, inspection and good practice that abound in the lifelong learning sector and then draws on the evidence of the 20 outstanding lessons to summa-rize what the 20 lessons had in common.

Through unique access to descriptions and analyses of these real les-sons, the book should provoke debate and encourage reflection. Inevitably, given the fact that all the lessons were outstanding, many themes recur and cut across those identified in the chapter headings. To address this, the book has a developmental structure and references are made in later chapters to lessons that have been described earlier on in the book. Readers who choose to adopt a **surface** approach might be tempted to dip into sections, but they are advised to read the book from beginning to end, to familiarize themselves with all 20 lessons, and to engage in some **deep** learning. There is more about deep and surface approaches to learning in the rest of the book.

2   Prudent planning

All 20 lessons were exceptionally well planned. It is clear that the teachers had thought very carefully about what they wanted their students to learn, how they were going to achieve this and how they would know whether or not they had been successful. This chapter will focus on four of these lessons. Before looking at each of these in detail, it is helpful to reflect on what they have in common in terms of planning.

Planning *what* to teach

Teachers in the lifelong learning sector rarely have any choice as to what to teach as this is usually determined by an externally set syllabus but they do, of course, plan which topics, concepts or themes to tackle in a given lesson.

In each of the four lessons, the teacher had completed a lesson plan, using the familiar model that has been adopted across the lifelong learning sector, as well as in schools and increasingly in higher education, whereby teachers construct a plan starting with aims and learning outcomes. This rational and linear approach, heavily influenced by Tyler (1949) and Bloom (1956), has remained the dominant lesson plan model for a long time, despite tweaks and changing emphases over the years. Its popularity may, as suggested by John (2006: 485), be as much to do with its 'elegant simplicity' as with the prevailing political climate with its focus on accountability. The questions raised by Tyler are still being asked today, for example 'how can we know if teachers have achieved their aims if they are not specified clearly in the first place?'

The relatively recent move towards a focus on learning, rather than teaching, as mentioned in Chapter 1, led to the replacement of objectives with outcomes. This, in turn, is linked to the shift from 'teacher-led' to 'student-centred' courses, modules and lessons. Objectives state what the teacher plans to cover, usually in terms of topics, and the associated assessment of these objectives focuses on how well students absorb the material taught. Learning outcomes, by the same token, articulate what students will be able to do by the end of the lesson and the assessment is designed to check this by providing opportunities for them to demonstrate what

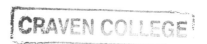

they have learned. Bloom's well-known taxonomy (1956) remains influential in relation to the formation and use of learning outcomes. The taxonomy divides learning into what appears to be an ascending hierarchy, from knowledge, comprehension and application to analysis, synthesis and evaluation. The verbs used in learning outcomes give an indication as to their level in the taxonomy. Examples of learning outcomes from the 20 outstanding lessons in this book are given in Table 2.1.

Further consideration of the impact of Bloom's work is given later in the book in relation to types of question and also in Chapter 7, when reviewing behaviourist approaches to teaching and learning.

Rarely contested in an explicit manner in the lifelong learning sector, this behaviourist, **outcomes-based** method of planning and practice is not

Table 2.1 Examples of learning outcomes used in the 20 lessons

Bloom's taxonomy	Students will be able to:
Knowledge	*recall* the stages involved in changing a carburettor (lesson 10) *list* the days of the week in English (lesson 11) *describe* materials used in basic bricklaying (lesson 18)
Comprehension	*explain* in their own words the meaning of 'standard deviation' (lesson 9) *identify* the main points in the article on reading with children (lesson 20) *explain* how they arrived at that calculation (lesson 8)
Application	*use* electrically powered cleaning equipment safely (lesson 16) *apply* punctuation correctly (lesson 3) *create* their own spreadsheet (lesson 17)
Analysis	*review* the planning policy and *debate* the issues it raises for their local community (lesson 4) *develop* ideas by investigating a range of relevant sources (lesson 7) *interpret* the client's brief (lesson 13)
Synthesis	*summarize* how humans see (lesson 2) *relate* the use of assessment criteria to their own subject/ practice (lesson 19) *draw* their own conclusions as to the key themes in the play (lesson 6)
Evaluation	*evaluate* their work placement (lesson 14) *reflect* on their work in the salon (lesson 15) *evaluate* their peers' presentations (lesson 12)

without its critics. Those who question its value or legitimacy in an educational setting (Farrell 2002; John 2006; Furedi 2012) suggest that learning outcomes are an attempt to monitor and quantify students' achievements and that this type of approach devalues the art of teaching and inhibits opportunities for teachers and students to experiment and explore. It can also reinforce a separation of learning from assessment and, in doing so, may neglect the significance of process. The extent to which this picture is reflected in the 20 outstanding lessons will be reviewed as the lessons are introduced and discussed.

With the demand to address in lesson plans so many seemingly additional factors, as mentioned in Chapter 1, the focus on what students are actually meant to learn can get lost. In recent years, lesson plans have incorporated references to various combinations of the following:

- learning styles
- differentiation
- personalization
- equality, diversity and inclusion
- use of information and communication technology
- targets
- 'Every Child Matters' themes
- safeguarding
- health and safety
- literacy
- numeracy
- team working
- enterprise.

In effect, some of the factors in this list are neither new nor additional. Differentiation, or mixed-ability teaching, inclusion and the development of skills, for example, have long been integral to good or outstanding teaching. What is relatively new is the requirement to be explicit about how each of these will be addressed.

Getting the learning outcomes right, at the planning stage, is critical. Too often, there is a temptation to pluck them arbitrarily from a syllabus or textbook. If they are too vague, general or content free, it is impossible to measure the extent to which they have been met. Contrariwise, narrow and highly specific outcomes may be too easy to measure and will therefore trivialize the purpose of the lesson.

What the four outstanding lessons in this chapter had in common, in terms of written lesson plans, was a minimalist approach but a strong sense of authenticity. The aims and outcomes were meaningful and written in plain English. They took into account what students already knew and could do, and they were used to guide, but not unduly constrain, the students and teacher. This was particularly the case for the last lesson, during which the experienced, confident and knowledgeable teacher decided to deviate from his plan, as will be explored later in this chapter.

Planning *how* to teach

The four lessons all centred on what is commonly referred to as **active** or **experiential** learning or 'learning by doing' (Dewey 1916; Gibbs 1988; Biggs 1999; Petty 2006). In the broadest sense, this means that students were participating in activities and speaking to each other and to the teacher, rather than observing or listening to someone else for the duration of the lesson. Involvement in authentic tasks provided them with the opportunity to make discoveries. Active or experiential learning is not at all uncommon in the lifelong learning sector and does not in itself constitute an outstanding, good or even satisfactory lesson. It is certainly not the case that *any* activity is better than a **didactic** approach to teaching. The activity needs to involve 'thinking' as well as 'doing'. Those who routinely observe lessons will be all too familiar with action-packed but content-light and intellectually weak lessons, as well as traditional, didactic lectures that can be highly stimulating and successful.

The activities in the four outstanding lessons were expertly designed and, in planning them, the teachers had taken into account the need to encourage students to take a *deep*, as opposed to *surface* approach to learning. Those who take a surface approach tend to focus on regurgitating facts or reproducing material for assessments, without the need or desire to understand what they have been taught. Research (Marton and Säljö 1976) suggests that while students may take different approaches to learning, these are not stable traits in an individual. The quality of teaching, therefore, has an impact on the approach students take to their learning. The characteristics associated with deep learning were evident in these four outstanding lessons, in that the students demonstrated they could link new ideas to their previous knowledge, relate concepts to their everyday experience and be motivated by interest rather than simply by assessment requirements. They were able to do this because the teachers of these outstanding lessons had provided structured opportunities for them to do so.

Motivation is widely recognized to be important for meaningful learning (Biggs 1999; Tavistock Institute 2002; Race 2005; Armitage et al. 2007). While teachers may have little or no impact on external factors that influence students, they do determine what happens in a lesson and, as will become clear, not all the students in the outstanding lessons described in this book were initially highly motivated to learn, even taking into account extrinsic factors such as the potential to gain qualifications and possibly a job or promotion. Motivation will be explored more fully in Chapter 5.

The lessons described below were dynamic, with constant review and adjustment by the teachers in light of whether or not they thought their students were learning what they had planned for them to learn. Ongoing assessment played an important part in this approach.

Planning assessment

It is common practice to advise teachers to avoid the word 'understand' in their learning outcomes on the basis that the measurement of under-standing is highly problematic (Knight and Yorke 2003). Similar arguments are made about using 'know', 'appreciate' and 'become familiar with' in learning outcomes. Developing students' understanding may well be the teacher's intention but, as suggested by Race et al. (2005), it is then neces-sary to be very clear about the depth of students' understanding expected and the evidence that students and the teacher would need to prove this.

In effect, assessment in the context of an outcomes-based system attempts to measure not understanding per se, but what students can do, say or produce *as a result of* their understanding. In the 20 outstand-ing lessons, teachers planned the use of a variety of assessment methods, including problem-solving tasks relating to everyday life, written exercises, observation, role play, discussion, presentations, peer marking and oral question and answer. In doing so, they provided students with opportuni-ties to demonstrate the impact of their understanding. Students were able, for example, to change a carburettor competently, lay bricks, explain to their peers how to look after a gerbil, articulate connections between a writer who ridiculed Athenian institutions more than 2000 years ago and modern-day politics or cut and blow-dry a client's hair. This would appear to support the trend outlined by the Tavistock Institute (2002) that in the post-modern educational institution, there has been a move away from perceiving knowledge as abstract towards that which is contextu-alized and often immediately applicable. This is likely to be even more prevalent in the lifelong learning sector, associated as it is primarily with vocational provision and work-based learning, than in either schools or higher education.

Educationalists distinguish between **formative** and **summative** assess-ment. Summative assessment relates to judgements made about an end product, usually resulting in a final mark or descriptor. Most often in the form of an essay, test, examination or portfolio, depending on the subject, it is used to grade, select and predict future performance. Formative assess-ment, by way of contrast, is the kind given during and between lessons to help students to know how well they are doing and what they need to do to improve. It also provides teachers with a measure of the effectiveness of their teaching. This reflects the idea of 'assessment *for* learning', as opposed to the summative notion of 'assessment *of* learning'. Formative assessment often comes in the form of written work marked by the teacher but it also plays a key role during lessons in terms of classroom interactions. This includes, for example, feedback by the teacher to students' responses to questions and contributions to discussions, as well as comments on tasks undertaken.

Highly effective formative assessment within a lesson does not happen by accident. In the four lessons in this chapter, it was subtle, sophisticated and planned, with the teacher regularly checking what students were doing, identifying potential problems and providing immediate feedback. 'Feedback is like fish' is an oft-used simile to emphasize the fact that feedback following assessment needs to be used quickly or it becomes useless. Many educationalists agree with Brown and Knight (1994) on the importance of giving students developmental formative feedback. Immediate, helpful and constructive formative feedback was integral to the teaching in these four lessons. It enabled the teachers to judge students' level of understanding and to adjust the content, pace and focus of the lesson accordingly.

Of particular note in these four lessons was the fact that the teachers very skilfully took the opportunity while students were working in groups or pairs to assess progress, coach, cajole and challenge individuals, rather than simply observe from afar or watch out for disruptive behaviour or distracting chat.

Planning the use of resources

A key resource in two of the lessons was the learning support worker or assistant. While the role of learning support assistants in the lifelong learning sector often lacks clarity (Bailey and Robson 2004), these two lessons highlight the success of very good teamwork between the different professionals. Not just 'an extra pair of hands', the learning support assistants' contribution was integral to the success of the lesson. Planning had very evidently involved the identification of the learning support assistants' role and specialist knowledge and skills. Students were clearly familiar with this pattern of working and benefited from the close working relationships between these professionals.

Three of the four lessons in this chapter highlight particularly creative and innovative use of learning resources. The fact that the other one had a limited range of additional resources serves to demonstrate that lessons do not have to have all the 'bells and whistles' to be outstanding, and that quality and relevance are more significant than quantity or variety.

Within the 20 outstanding lessons, there were examples of how teachers had planned the use of their material not just to support the intended topic or subject but also to highlight associated issues around equality and diversity. Not only were the materials used attractively produced and devoid of spelling and grammatical errors, they also reflected cultural diversity in terms of names, locations and images. The planning policy in the geography lesson, discussed later in this chapter, for example, was used very effectively to draw attention to the needs, views and perceptions of the socially and ethnically diverse communities in the locality. Other ways in which teachers promoted diversity are discussed in Chapter 6.

Four outstanding lessons

Although any of the 20 lessons could have been used, the four selected for this chapter are useful examples in that they are all different in style, format and context. The first was based around one main creatively designed numeracy task, but with carefully planned opportunities for individuals to focus on developing specific knowledge and skills. In the second, located in a science laboratory, students worked on different activities to do with vision, moving from one activity to another in turn. In contrast to these two lessons, each adult evening class learner in the third lesson worked on different tasks tailored to their own specific literacy or numeracy requirements for most of the time. In the final lesson, on urban population growth, in a sixth-form college, the teacher chose to deviate from his well-considered plan, seizing an opportunity in the lesson to take a slightly different direction and to initiate a whole-group discussion.

Lesson 1

Subject – numeracy
Course/level – entry
Lesson length – 90 minutes
Location – further education college
Number of students present – eight
Age – 16 to 24
Context – full-time course; all students with moderate learning difficulties and/or
    disabilities; 4 female and 4 male; 1 learning support assistant

The lesson started promptly with very little in the way of introduction by the teacher. She gathered the students around a flip chart and asked them to explain the meaning of words and phrases such as 'add', 'take away', 'subtract', 'multiply', 'divide', 'increase', 'decrease', 'reduce', 'rise', 'fall', 'greater than', 'less than', 'enlarge', 'extend', 'expand', 'decline', 'contract' and 'augment'. The students answered the easier ones confidently and, as they came to the more unfamiliar terms, they acknowledged that they did not know the meaning and so they themselves suggested checking in a dictionary. Unprompted, three students used dictionaries successfully and fed back the answers to the rest of the group. This was all done within the first ten minutes of the lesson.

While the learning support assistant supervised a short quiz with the students on the interactive whiteboard that reinforced their understanding of these new terms, the teacher set up the room, with one large cardboard box of stationery on each of the four tables. The main task required each pair of students, carefully selected to work with each other, to help the teacher check a delivery sent to the college. They were asked to make sure that the contents of their stationery box matched the information on the piece of paper provided by the supplier of the stationery. The contents of the boxes varied. For example, some had just individual items, such as pens and erasers, while others had packs of 20 pencils. Consequently, the complexity of the tasks varied to accommodate different levels of challenge for each pair of students.

Students worked enthusiastically and purposefully, checking their own orders and helping their partners, keen to ensure accuracy. After 30 minutes, the teacher asked for feedback and each of the four pairs reported mistakes made by the supplier. The teacher wrote these errors on the whiteboard, using the terms they had explored earlier. She very skilfully encouraged students to use them too, with questions like 'So, do we need to get the supplier to *increase* or *decrease* the number of notepads . . . and by how much?' 'Should we *subtract* or add that amount?' The questions were adjusted appropriately to align to each individual student's level, challenging but not embarrassing them.

Once all the mistakes were listed, the teacher asked what they should do next. In the majority of cases, the supplier had overcharged the college. However, there was an amusing discussion about whether or not they should be honest where, in a few instances, the supplier had undercharged them. The students suggested calling the supplier and when asked how they could find out the telephone number several students excitedly pointed out that it was on the invoice.

The teacher handed her mobile telephone to one of the students and, although initially anxious about the prospect of making a call, he agreed. He rang the number and a college technician in a nearby room answered, already primed to play the role of the supplier. The student accurately explained the details of the errors using the newly acquired terminology. The rest of the group were genuinely proud of him and the fact that he successfully negotiated a revised invoice. Finishing exactly on time at this point, the teacher thanked the group for their hard work.

Commentary

This lesson was meticulously planned. The overall aim was related to developing students' knowledge and skills around addition, subtraction, multiplication and division.

Rather than say 'today you will learn . . .', the teacher described the task they would undertake in terms of helping her with a job she had to do. This task was astutely devised to develop students' conceptual understanding of numeracy in a purposeful and realistic context. By doing so, she kept the whole group together, giving the lesson a sense of momentum and fun, but at the same time she provided opportunities for each student to be challenged by working on specific tasks matched to their ability.

What did these students learn? The lesson incorporated very specific measurable outcomes relating to mathematical concepts for each student. These individual outcomes were met. They were stated for each student on cards on their table and checked unobtrusively by the teacher or learning support assistant while the students were working in pairs. However, the lesson was about much more than this. As well as making progress in the development of their numeracy knowledge and skills, the students thoroughly enjoyed themselves. This had a demonstrable impact on their attitude to mathematics as well as to their capability in manipulating numbers. It is more than likely that the knowledge and skills that students assimilated in this lesson would be applied in a practical way in the immediate future. In addition, what students learned provided a solid foundation on which to build for further, more complex work in mathematics at a later stage.

This lesson is a good example of cooperative working and highlights the importance of learning in a social context and through interaction with other students as well as with the teacher. The students were not just working in pairs. The design of the task meant that they really felt they were all depending on each other to get it right.

Lesson 2

Subject – human anatomy and physiology
Course/level – GCSE
Lesson length – two hours
Location – further education college
Number of students present – 18
Age – adults
Context – part-time course; 11 female and 7 male; 1 learning support assistant

The aim of this lesson was for learners to gain knowledge about the anatomy of the human eye in relation to its function. The teacher started the lesson promptly and dealt effectively, and unobtrusively, with a few latecomers.

The first five minutes involved a recap of the previous lesson on hearing, which learners participated in enthusiastically, demonstrating good recall and understanding.

The teacher then very skilfully asked learners questions about vision to ascertain their existing knowledge, having provided them with mini-whiteboards for their written or drawn responses. This was all completed promptly and 15 minutes into the lesson the learners moved on to the main activity.

Learners were invited to participate, in turn, in a series of activities already laid out in the laboratory. One activity was a large model of the human eye with notes and a diagram for learners to label. Another dealt with finding the blind spot, with questions to help learners make sense of this phenomenon. A torch and a series of tasks provided learners with the opportunity to illustrate the role of the iris when compared to the iris diaphragm of an old camera. A set of colour blindness diagnostic cards encouraged learners to ask and answer some thought-provoking questions. Two ray boxes and convex and concave lenses, supported by notes and questions for learners to answer, facilitated discussion on short and long sight and the role of corrective lenses. Students also watched a brief video clip to show the arrangement of rods and cones in the eye and an arresting set of optical illusions on a computer and this generated productive discussions.

These activities were cleverly designed to relate to each other and to provide different ways in which learners could investigate the structures in the eye and to contribute to their understanding of sight. Learners were completely absorbed by the activities and engaged in animated conversations, with each other and with the teacher. This included two Somalian learners, who benefited from sensitive and highly effective assistance with their use and understanding of English from the learning support assistant.

The learners' written work demonstrated their ability to apply their understanding of sight and where appropriate during the lesson, the teacher and learning support assistant corrected spelling and grammatical errors. In doing this, they took time to ensure that students understood errors so that they were less likely to make the same mistakes again in the future.

Commentary

This was another superbly planned lesson, employing experiential learning. These adults learned by doing. It was clear as they participated in each activity that, to quote one of the learners, 'things fell into place' as they began to understand more about vision. The teacher made very effective use of what is known as an **'advance organizer'** (Ausubel 1960) which is, in effect, information provided to help students to organize what comes next. The teacher did this by enabling the learners to bridge the gap between what they already knew, which she established through a short activity at the start of the lesson and what they were about to learn. She set the lesson in context, explaining how each of the activities they would participate in would contribute to their understanding. She directed attention to what would be most important and she highlighted the relationships between the activities. In using an advance organizer, she helped the learners to organize the new information in a way that would give them a better chance of understanding and remembering it.

A variety of assessment methods were used, as linked to each of the activities there were notes to read, short questions to answer, diagrams to label and multiple choice quizzes to complete. Through observation, discussion, checking written answers and questioning, the teacher maintained a strong handle on what learners were grasping, what they found difficult and when it was necessary to intervene with questions and explanations. In doing so, she provided learners with excellent feedback. On several occasions she encouraged learners to explain concepts to one another, to minimize her own involvement. The teacher's planning of how to structure the lesson, lay out the laboratory and use the resources, including the learning support assistant, were exemplary and led to a highly successful lesson.

What did these students learn? To refer back to the second definition of learning in Chapter 1, it was evident that, for these individuals, there was indeed a 'significant change' in their knowledge and understanding. As the lesson progressed, the learners gradually assimilated new knowledge and made sense of it. By the end, they were not simply able to recite how the eye functions and the brain moderates the messages to produce sight, they could also explain it clearly and convincingly in their own words, demonstrating a real depth of understanding.

Lesson 3

Subject – skills for life (literacy and numeracy)
Course/level – various
Lesson length – two hours
Location – community centre
Number of students present – eight
Age – adults
Context – part-time course; 6 female and 2 male

This lesson took place in the evening. Not untypically for this type of provision, the learners were at varying levels and had different reasons for attending the lesson. For example, one young woman needed mathematics at a certain level to get onto a teacher training course. Another woman wanted to be able to help her children with their homework, but she 'couldn't do maths at school'. An older man needed to be able to read information at work and an unemployed young man wanted to improve his English and acquire some qualifications in order to secure a job.

Learners, who clearly knew each other well, arrived early and chatted with each other. The lesson got off to a brisk start and the teacher introduced a lively series of introductory exercises, which involved all learners asking and answering questions relating to both literacy and numeracy. These drew on the learners' lives, for example addressing issues around shopping, the weather forecast, bus and train timetables, ages and birthdays. To pull these activities together, the teacher made extremely skilful use of targeted questions, clearly differentiated to accommodate each individual's level and interest.

After this group activity, the learners reminded themselves and each other about what they were working on, referring to their own individual plans. Some then retrieved resources from a cupboard in the room that included laptop computers, cards, dice, jigsaws, cubes, wooden letters, photographs and newspapers. Others had brought in their own learning resources from home. They all started to organize themselves and then settled down to working productively and independently.

The teacher circulated, offering advice and further resources, with comments such as: 'Let's pick up on where we left off last week with some follow-up work on measurement . . .' or 'As we discussed last week, you want to do some more work on speaking and listening. Use these headphones and listen to this interesting debate on transport policies and the environment. See what you think – it is quite controversial. How might you respond to the viewpoints expressed by each of the participants?'

The atmosphere in the room was industrious, with learners working very purposefully and enthusiastically on tailor-made tasks. The teacher was very careful to avoid a situation in which the learners would become dependent on her. In asking and answering questions, she encouraged them to think through possible responses and to come up with their own solutions. In doing so, she was not afraid of pauses and silence while the learners gathered their thoughts. However, the teacher did not shy away from providing learners with constructive feedback, where appropriate, to help them understand what they had done well but also where they had made mistakes and why. She ensured learners were able to use this feedback to inform what they would be tackling next.

At the end of the lesson, she brought the learners together for a quick recap of what they had achieved and confirmation of what they would each need to do in the following lesson.

Commentary

The combination of mixed-ability and mixed-subject teaching, not uncommon for skills for life lessons, can be very daunting for a teacher. Many also involve English for speakers of other languages, as well as literacy and numeracy. However, in this exceptionally well-planned lesson, the teacher very skilfully balanced the provision of one-to-one specialist support and appropriate challenge for individuals with ensuring that they felt that they belonged to a group. As is so typical of adult education, this encouraged learners to provide one another with mutual support. The teacher demonstrated considerable expertise in the teaching of both literacy and numeracy and was comfortable working at all levels in both subjects. The criticality of this kind of pedagogical subject-specialist knowledge is discussed in the next chapter.

This approach would not have been so successful had the teacher not spent weeks prior to this lesson encouraging learners to take the initiative to work productively on their own. Such independent learning has to be carefully planned. As in previous lessons with this group, the teacher had recognized the stage each learner was at, provided appropriate material relevant to their everyday life and encouraged and prompted them to move on to the next level. The **scaffolding** provided at each point in the process was allowing her to gradually withdraw support as the learners became more independent. This type of scaffolding is often associated with the work of Vygotsky (1962), who is widely known for what he called the 'zone of proximal development'. At its simplest, this is the difference between what learners can do without help and what they can do with help. Although focused on the relationship between an adult and a child, it is as applicable to the work of teachers in both the lifelong learning and higher education sectors.

There is a temptation to assume that this type of lesson is easy to teach, in that all the learners are highly motivated and so they can each be given something 'to get on with'. This is not the case and this teacher focused on high expectations for all learners and the development of their independent learning skills. She did not, as is too often the case with adult learners, emphasize the benefits of soft skills such as confidence and self-esteem, important though they are, over and above the intended knowledge learners were expected to acquire.

What did these students learn? Each individual made very good progress against specific and measurable learning outcomes. The impact of these relatively 'small' achievements each lesson, made possible by the excellent teaching and mutually supportive environment, was that these learners had realized that they were able to overcome previous barriers to learning. Mastery of these essential skills had eluded them in the past. The fact that they could now work independently and successfully had resulted in a significant change in their attitudes, values and capabilities, as well as their knowledge and understanding of literacy and/or numeracy.

Lesson 4

Subject – geography
Course/level – AS level
Lesson length – 90 minutes
Location – sixth-form college
Number of students present – 16
Age – 17 to 18
Context – full-time course; 9 female and 7 male

The subject of this lesson was urban population growth and the politics and economics behind housing policies at local and national government level. Using his knowledge of the local area in which these students lived, the teacher set out a hypothetical planning policy from central government requiring the local council to build a large number of new homes in the town. Within minutes of starting the lesson, the teacher asked students to confer in pairs and to put forward, with justifications, their proposals.

Students started to work on the task in hand, with varying degrees of enthusiasm and understanding, and the teacher dropped in on each discussion to gauge the contributions being made. This was the part of the lesson in which he could ascertain the degree to which individual students engaged with the task and the different ways in which they responded. It was clear that such an open-ended exercise would prompt very different levels of response and further inform the teacher's approach.

As the teacher walked around the room and listened to what his students were saying, he became aware that several dialogues were becoming quite personal and social prejudices were starting to lead students' decision-making. The discussion was becoming quite heated in some quarters. It was still relevant to the topic, but animated and clouded by personality and subjectivity.

Adjusting his plan at this stage, the teacher chose to open up for his students the much more elemental questions of why people choose to live where they do, what sort of people and landscape they want around them and just what it is to be a neighbour. The class discussion that followed was lively and deftly managed by the teacher. With students fired up by the realization that they all had things to say about people from different neighbourhoods near where they lived, the teacher took the calculated risk of chairing a whole-class discussion about what should guide local housing development in their own town.

In fact, it turned out to be not too much of a risk in that he cleverly smuggled into the discussion and onto the whiteboard historical principles, current practices and political issues that would be all the more memorable because of the association students would make with their own energetic discussion. He managed the debate expertly, skilfully taking something said by one student and, with a bit of rephrasing, offering it back to the class for further comment. He took every opportunity to impart new knowledge, using questions and timely interventions to teach his students things they did not already know. They absorbed this alongside what their peers were saying and he made sure that, at key points, he summarized core arguments, recapitulated where these ideas had come from and why they carried weight. He reminded students that they could now not only rehearse these arguments themselves but illustrate them from their own personal experience.

At the end of the lesson, students commented on how quickly the time had passed, expressing disappointment that the debate had to finish. They continued discussing the topic with one another as they left the room.

Commentary

This was an adventurously stimulating lesson in which the teacher had the confidence and skill to deviate from his lesson plan in order to accommodate the responses made by his students, ensuring that they remained in a questioning, exploratory state of mind throughout the lesson and so were exceptionally receptive to what he wanted them to learn. Of all the 20 lessons, this one stands out as being the most focused on process, rather than outcome.

Teachers often face a situation in which, as in this lesson, students say things that are considered to be inappropriate. In this instance, the teacher realized that students were becoming too personal and were basing their decisions on prejudices he considered to be of concern. The safe choice would have been to defuse any personal animosity speedily and steer students through to more objective and detached perspectives. However, this teacher decided to embrace what was happening among the students and work it into the scope of the debate, with the ultimate aim of achieving the former objective of detachment. He trusted his instincts and experience in judging this to be a more creative and rewarding choice. Some teachers might have struggled to hold this together, but this was an accomplished practitioner who knew his material inside out and knew where to draw the line when it came to exposing students' prejudices in front of their friends, often using humour to prevent the atmosphere from getting too fraught.

What did these students learn? They learned what the teacher had planned to impart to them, in terms of information about urban population growth, politics, economics and the roles of local and national government in relation to housing policies. Students also learned how to marshal facts and evidence to support a case and how better to construct an argument. In an unusually explicit manner, there was clear evidence of significant changes in attitudes and values, as students questioned and challenged the teacher, one another and even themselves, about established viewpoints, prejudices and evidence-based decision-making.

Although these students had chosen this subject to study, not all of them were intrinsically motivated by the topic or the desire to learn for the sake of it. The teacher was aware of this and had decided to try to motivate them by conducting an exercise that would bring home to them, in ways that might touch their daily lives, the significance and complexity of decisions about where people might choose or be able to live in a crowded country.

Chapter summary

Prudent planning was central to the success of these four lessons – and indeed to the next 16, too, as will be evident in future chapters. The teachers all made astute choices as to how best they could use the time they had with their students. The topics to be covered, the teaching methods and the assessment tasks were all carefully aligned to complement each other. Teachers' thoughtful planning ensured that resources, including the learning support assistants, were used to very good effect to support students. There was little if any opportunity in these stimulating lessons for students to lose interest or become disruptive. Students remained motivated throughout the lessons, in no small part due to the passion and enthusiasm of their teachers.

Lesson summary (lessons 1–4)

Table 2.2   Lesson summary (lessons 1–4)

	Particular strengths
Lesson 1 Numeracy	• Meticulous planning • Very good development of students' mathematical skills, as a consequence of innovative problem-solving task, used well to maintain interest, to be fun and to be collaborative • High expectations and participation of all students, regardless of level, learning difficulty or disability • Superb classroom management skills • Excellent use of learning support assistant • Excellent use of guided **discovery learning**

(continued)

Table 2.2   Lesson summary (lessons 1–4) (*continued*)

	Particular strengths
Lesson 2 Human anatomy and physiology	• Very thorough planning • Very clear evidence of learners grasping the information and main concepts to be learned • Skilfully devised and implemented learning opportunities • Excellent resources, used to very good effect • Expert classroom management • Excellent use of learning support assistant • Particularly constructive formative feedback by teacher • Very good literacy and language support
Lesson 3 Skills for life	• Outstanding planning, with tailor-made tasks for each learner • Considerable progress made by each learner • High level of independent learning • Creative tasks at appropriate levels to challenge each learner • Highly inclusive, supportive and industrious environment created • High level of subject knowledge in both literacy and numeracy by teacher • Excellent formative feedback by teacher
Lesson 4 Geography	• Excellent planning • Clear evidence of students developing their reasoning skills and reflecting on their own outlook and views • Superb questioning skills and management of discussion by passionate and enthusiastic teacher • Excellent classroom management skills that maintained momentum and prevented any disruption • Outstanding approach to challenging prejudice

3 Passion and enthusiasm

The words *passion* and *enthusiasm* rarely, if ever, appear in observation checklists or lesson plans and yet they are often perceived to be the bedrock of highly successful lessons. These characteristics were not necessarily conveyed in the outstanding lessons in the form of exceptionally flamboyant, emotional or extravert teachers, but rather in their considerable subject expertise, infectious enthusiasm and obvious desire to share this with their students.

It is difficult to reflect this type of atmosphere in a lesson plan. Discussion in the previous chapter focused on various aspects of planning, but teachers do not explicitly plan to be passionate or enthusiastic in a lesson. Cynics might argue that teachers may be tempted to take this approach when they are being observed but, as noted in one of the myths in Chapter 8, unexpected or significant changes in a teacher's behaviour are transparent to both the students and the observer. It is much easier, of course, to measure the extent to which students achieve the intended learning outcomes in a lesson than it is to ascertain the level or value of a teacher's passion and enthusiasm.

Research

Anecdotal evidence suggests that people remember 'inspirational' teachers and this is supported to some degree by research. For example, the importance of teachers' enthusiasm and passion is highlighted by Tedder and Lawy (2010) who, in a study on mentoring in the lifelong learning sector, draw attention to the fact that these two qualities are prominent in the narratives of their interviews with trainees, tutors and managers about the people who inspired them. There are similar findings in relation to teachers' passion in the school sector (Fried 1995; Day 2009). Day (2009) draws on a comparative study of policies aimed at improving teaching in New Zealand, Italy, America, Sweden and France to highlight that excellent teachers in these countries had a passionate desire for the success of all their students. He also argues that passion should not be regarded only as a fixed disposition and that it can diminish as well as grow. In outlining the ways in which passionate teachers approach their teaching, Fried (1995) highlights core values, attitudes and respectful relationships, most of which are reflected in the outstanding lessons in this book. In higher education, various studies, albeit small scale (Little et al. 2007), found that both teachers' and students' perceptions of teaching excellence emphasize teachers' personal qualities, most notably enthusiasm and inspiration. In identifying the properties of good teaching, from the teacher's point of view, Ramsden (2003: 86) puts 'the desire to share a love of the subject with students' as the first in a list. Glasner (2003) argues that while outstanding teachers are passionate in the pursuit of enabling others to learn, they do not operate in a vacuum but develop and grow within a supportive environment. The extent and nature of the influence of institutional culture on teachers' practice is an interesting topic for further research and exploration.

Subject expertise

As well as displaying passion, enthusiasm and excellent generic teaching skills, the teachers of the 20 outstanding lessons demonstrated that they knew their subjects in depth and how to teach them exceptionally well.

In the hospitality, construction, cleaning and support services, media studies, art and design, hairdressing and motor vehicle studies lessons, these dual professionals presented themselves as expert practitioners in their own field as well as highly skilled teachers. Through their expertise and enthusiasm for their subjects and the high expectations they had of their students to produce work of a professional standard, they engendered a strong sense of loyalty and pride among their cohorts.

To socialize students into their discipline, the teachers adopted an ethos associated with the relevant profession in the workplace, be it a kitchen, salon, studio, workshop or computer suite. They strove to inculcate core habits that clearly motivated students to aspire to high standards. The teachers were not just developing students' practical skills and ability to use technical terminology correctly. They were also helping students to develop the kind of tacit knowledge about a discipline that is hard to put into words but easier to demonstrate.

There is considerable research suggesting that learning is particularly effective when it is relevant and meaningful, includes authentic activities and is set in an appropriate context (Dewey 1916; Vygotsky 1978; Brown et al. 1989; Lave and Wenger 1991). The type of traditional apprenticeship model, whereby students acquire skills and explicit and tacit knowledge through observation, imitation and practice, has not changed significantly over decades and even centuries. The teachers of these outstanding lessons were applying what some educationalists refer to as cognitive apprentice-ship models (Brown et al. 1989). This involves modelling, coaching, scaf-folding, fading, reflection and exploration in a way that enables students to apply their skills in a range of contexts. These phases will be explored further in the commentaries on the outstanding lessons in this chapter as well as in future chapters.

Induction into the relevant disciplinary discourse was also evident in the science, humanities, arts and social science lessons, where the teachers were similarly knowledgeable and passionate about their own subjects. As in the vocational lessons, these teachers knew how to organize their subject and how to stage the introduction of important ideas, concepts and skills, in a way that would bridge the distance between what students understood and what counted as key knowledge in the discipline. This was very evi-dent in the skills for life lesson in the previous chapter, where the teacher's expertise in both literacy and numeracy enabled her to close that gap with her learners with significant precision.

The debate about generic and discipline-specific expertise raises a question about the extent to which subject-specialist pedagogy features in teacher education courses for the lifelong learning sector, which has been a thorny issue for some time. Most courses are generic and offer trainees opportunities to apply general educational theory to their own practice through placement or research projects and assignments. In the secondary school sector, it is different in that trainees undertake a discipline-specific course, whereby they study both their subject and the associated pedagogy. This approach has been replicated in the lifelong learning sector for skills for life subjects, primarily as a result of concerns about student outcomes in numeracy, literacy and ESOL and teachers' expertise in these subjects. It is more difficult, though, to adopt such an approach for the rest of this highly complex and diverse sector with its five distinct segments, as identified in Chapter 1. The sector caters for school pupils, further and higher education students, apprentices, employees and adult learners, with a huge array of subjects, ranging from yoga, floristry and manicure to health and social care, automotive engineering and philosophy.

Structure, insight and patterns

The importance of grasping the structure of a subject was central to Bruner's influential work (1960, 1966) on teaching and learning. He described the sense of excitement of discovery as the structure of a discipline becomes clear to students. They are made aware of the patterns in a subject and how certain ideas come up again and again and can be applied in new ways. Each subject has its own structure and big ideas and the teachers of outstanding lessons demonstrated that they were particularly good at enabling students to see how these ideas fitted together so that they could make sense of it all.

When the teacher organizes the content and sequence of what students learn to maximize comprehension in this way, it is usually referred to as *discovery, inquiry-based* or *problem-based learning*. If they do so to orchestrate 'eureka' moments, when the penny drops, this is known as *insight learning*, as espoused by Gestaltists (Kohler 1925). This German school of psychology argued that the nature of the parts is determined by, and is secondary to, the whole. So, when they gain these insights, students feel as if the pieces of what they are trying to learn fit together into a pattern. Indeed, *Gestalt* is the German word for pattern. This may appear to be easier to apply in some subjects, such as science, mathematics and information technology, but it is also possible in the arts, social sciences and humanities, even with abstract concepts.

These approaches were successfully adopted in the lessons described in the previous chapter. Students in the human anatomy and physiology lesson, for example, were delighted as they realized how each of the well-designed activities they completed fitted together to help them to deepen their understanding of how the human eye functions. Through expert questioning, students in the geography lesson began to appreciate not just the many factors and differing viewpoints involved in urban planning, but also the extent to which they could formulate an argument more cogently.

Students working on the numeracy tasks in the first lesson in Chapter 2 were motivated to continue as they saw certain patterns emerge. One of the students with learning difficulties, for example, was genuinely excited when he realized there were two ways in which he could check the number of printer cartridges to make sure that the college was paying the correct amount for this particular purchase. First, he counted them all individually and then he checked by multiplying the number of packets by the number of printer cartridges in each packet.

In the same lesson, the teacher very cleverly developed students' understanding of the term 'invoice'. She asked, early on in the lesson, if anyone knew what an invoice was. No hands went up and only one student guessed, suggesting it might be 'a message left on a mobile phone'. The teacher left this question unresolved. Later on, after the students had completed the main activity, she asked the same question again. All the students put their hands up. The way in which the students answered the question this time illustrated a real and *deep* understanding because they had discovered the answer themselves, having each seen, used and checked their products against an invoice. Had they simply been given a definition, or even shown real examples without an associated activity, they may have realized what it was but they would not have been as confident in their understanding and they would have been less likely to remember it.

Four outstanding lessons

The four lessons in this chapter reflect in different ways the passion, enthusiasm and expertise of the teachers. One is a practical hospitality lesson, taught in a kitchen, with students preparing meals for real, paying customers. A quite different lesson reflects a seemingly traditional approach to the teaching of A level classical civilization in a sixth-form college. The third is a practical physics lesson focused on examination revision, taught by an enthusiastic physicist, and the final lesson is art and design, with students industriously developing their own creative artefacts in a studio.

Lesson 5

Subject – hospitality
Course/level – intermediate
Lesson length – four hours
Location – further education college
Number of students present – 15
Age – 16 to 18
Context – full-time course; 4 female and 11 male

In the college's main kitchen, students prepared ballotines, stuffed boneless legs of chicken, for the college refectory. Preparing a ballotine has a number of useful relevant processes for students to learn. These include removing the sinews from the bird's legs, cutting the legs from the carcass, removing the bone from the leg, the preparation of forcemeat from chicken's leg meat and finally stuffing and sewing up the boneless leg.

The teacher started the lesson by explaining what students would be doing and learning, based on a relevant and succinct lesson plan. The teacher provided short demonstrations of each process to the students. These were sufficiently detailed to show the procedure, but not so long that students failed to remember the different parts of the process. In addition, during each demonstration the teacher reinforced previous learning topics on chicken, for example the risk of contamination. Responses to the teacher's clear questions, targeted at specific individuals, confirmed that students were listening and had grasped key concepts and processes. A discussion on halal and kosher methods of slaughtering chicken provoked a genuine curiosity among the students about different cultures. They clearly felt comfortable asking questions and admitting that they did not know much about different religions.

After every demonstration, the students returned to their benches to work at the skill the teacher had shown them. The teacher then moved round the kitchen reinforcing information and supporting each student, depending on his or her different skill level. Those attaining the skills quickly moved on to the next stage, but for students needing more time to develop skills the teacher helped with detailed explanations and, if appropriate, further demonstrations of particular techniques. After the completion of the ballotines, the teacher reviewed the students' work, the different processes involved in production, as well as the different uses, definitions, spellings and visual images of ballotines.

In a lesson on kitchen calculations, later the same day, the teacher went through the costs of making the ballotines with the students. Students undertook the relevant calculations with appropriate accuracy and speed to demonstrate how much the college refectory had needed to charge to cover costs and make a small profit.

Commentary

In this very well-planned and tightly managed lesson, the teacher's passion shone through as he very skilfully undertook short demonstrations and reinforced different techniques. He was sufficiently confident in his catering knowledge and teaching ability to know that he would be able to get each student to prepare 20 ballotines of chicken, so that they could meet the college's need to have 300 of this particular dish for lunch that day.

The teacher was applying what might be described as the cognitive apprenticeship model, as discussed earlier in this chapter. He modelled the task so that students could observe him. He coached the students by observing them and offering support, but in a way that allowed each student to assume as much of the task as she or he could manage. The 'fading' phase involved the gradual removal of support as the lesson progressed and students were completing the tasks on their own.

What did these students learn? Clearly, they mastered the skill of preparing and cooking a ballotine of chicken. The fact that they were required to do this a further 19 times meant that they were able to demonstrate the specific techniques very effectively, with appropriate speed and with confidence. Often, in hospitality lessons, students prepare only one or two of any dish, so they acquire the relevant knowledge and skill but do not have the opportunity to practise so intensely. Because of the way in which the teacher took time to question, guide, explore and reflect, the students were also able to demonstrate an understanding of what they were doing and why. In terms of a change in their practice, capability and attitudes, they learned how to think and work like experts. This played a part in bringing the 'tricks of the trade' type of tacit knowledge into the students' consciousness so that it became more explicit.

This lesson was another example of cooperative learning. Although students worked on their own, unlike the other example of cooperative learning where students worked in pairs, there was an atmosphere of collegiality in the kitchen as all the students were relying on one another to produce food of a high standard. Both social learning theory, associated mostly with Bandura (1986), and situated learning theories (Lave and Wenger 1991) are relevant here. The former focuses on the fact that people learn from observing others around them, while the latter is about learning that takes place in the same setting in which it is applied. The context in which this lesson took place, in a 'workplace' with the pressing need to meet the demands of paying customers, played an integral part in determining what and how students learned. Under the supervision of this passionate chef, the students were enthusiastic about what they were learning, and the idea of not cooperating, appearing to lack motivation or misbehaving was simply not an option for them.

Lesson 6

Subject – classical civilization
Course/level – A level
Lesson length – one hour
Location – sixth-form college
Number of students present – eight
Age – 17 to 19
Context – full-time course; 2 female and 6 male

After a very brief introduction and recap of what students had learned in the previous lesson, the teacher wasted no time in getting to the heart of the lesson, which was a detailed discussion between teacher and students of *The Wasps* by Aristophanes.

The teacher guided the discussion through a combination of excellent questioning techniques supported by elaboration and explication where appropriate. Although he did not focus explicitly on syllabus or assessment requirements, the teacher very skilfully developed students' intellectual curiosity in a way that would prepare them well for their forthcoming examination. Throughout the lesson, he used humour judiciously to promote a depth of understanding and to create a positive attitude to the subject.

The students had prepared thoroughly for the lesson, reflecting both high levels of motivation and an awareness of this teacher's demanding expectations of them. In addition to reading the relevant material beforehand, they had participated during the week in an online discussion among themselves on the college's virtual learning environment, debating the extent to which Aristophanes had serious targets in *The Wasps* or whether he was just trying to make the audience laugh.

The teacher was well aware of each student's capacity and potential and used this information to tailor questions and expectations accordingly.

For example, he asked certain individuals to explain their thinking clearly for the benefit of those who found specific aspects, themes or topics more difficult to comprehend. All students participated in the discussion and most asked as well as answered questions. To bring the subject alive and to place classical civilization in a context that students could make sense of, the teacher was adept at linking the drama of Aristophanes to aspects of modern culture. This included reference to both contemporary politics and soap opera storylines. This approach was successful in strengthening, rather than compromising, students' understanding of the historical context of the play. Throughout, all students were both animated and fascinated, demonstrating enjoyment and a thirst for learning.

The teacher concluded the lesson by directing students to relevant material on the college's virtual learning environment, giving homework and confirming times for individual tutorials, at which he would discuss their most recent essay.

Commentary

This lesson reflects the traditional 'chalk and talk' approach to teaching and learning, considered by many in the sector to be old fashioned. Forthcoming examinations may well have been in the minds of the teacher and students, but this lesson stands out among the others as the one most likely to be associated with the liberal tradition of education for self-development. One could reasonably argue that this approach is only successful with highly motivated students. The inter-relationship, though, between motivation and teaching and learning is not straightforward, as will be discussed more fully in Chapter 5. It may well be that these students had become even more motivated over the last few months because they had had this inspirational, passionate and extremely knowledgeable teacher. In this particular case, with these students and this teacher, the choice of teaching approach worked extremely well.

What did these students learn? They not only deepened their understanding of the play through listening to the teacher and to their peers and by contributing to the discussion, they also learned more about the political and military events that took place around the time of its production. In debating points of view, students developed their analytical skills and their ability to present a cogent argument, informed by appropriate evidence.

Although it appeared to have been a fairly informal lesson, the teacher had planned it carefully to ensure that students had undertaken the relevant preparation. By setting up the online discussion group, he knew the students would not let one another down by not participating. Their contributions throughout the week had given him a clear indication as to their level of understanding and where the gaps were in their knowledge. He used this information subtly in the lesson, as he directed questions and comments to particular individuals.

Lesson 7

Subject – art and design
Course/level – advanced
Lesson length – two and a half hours
Location – further education college
Number of students present – 14
Age – 16 to 18
Context – full-time course; 15 female and 3 male

The lesson was part of a one-week project on the theme of light. The teacher had asked students to produce a sketchbook showing their ideas and development and also to produce a final piece in their chosen discipline – for example, three-dimensional, painting, textiles, fashion, graphics or sculpture.

The students had arrived early and the studio soon became a hive of activity, with everyone working industriously on their individual interpretations of the brief they had been given. To stimulate ideas and to provide students with something tangible as a starting point to work on, the teacher had set out a range of materials, each with light reflecting or transparent qualities. These were draped in the studio and lit with spotlights. Some students painted or sketched, some used fabrics, cellophane papers and foils on stands to create garments, while others generated three-dimensional constructions involving shadows and reflections.

The teacher circulated around the group to gauge progress and to listen to students, who explained what their next steps could be. Students were enthusiastic and able to talk about how they had developed their own ideas. The teacher entered into a professional dialogue with each of them, offering sensitive but constructively critical feedback, and remaining silent at times to give students the opportunity to think and reflect and to come up with alternative approaches themselves, where appropriate. She alerted them to work by specific artists from different cultures that might inspire them further and directed them to the library of art books she maintained in the corner of the studio.

In their sketchbooks, students had recorded fully each stage of their experimentation. It was clear that these students, all of whom were planning to go on to higher education, were achieving the self-confidence and creative independence they needed for that next stage in their studies. Students were reluctant to leave the studio at the end of the lesson.

Commentary

Very different to the hospitality lesson, where all students were undertaking the same task within a highly structured context, and to the classical civilization example, which was focused around a whole-group
discussion, these art students all worked at their own pace on individual
projects. It was clear to students that the *process* of learning in this lesson
was as important, if not more so, as the product in terms of students' final
pieces.

A key strength of the lesson was the way in which the teacher used
her time, enthusiasm and expertise while students were working on their
own. She provided excellent feedback – and 'feed forward' – to ensure that
students were learning to become reflective practitioners themselves and
also to encourage them to strive for high standards of work. She did this
through the skilful use of question and answer, often pausing after each
question to give students enough thinking time. She interspersed this with
statements about aspects of students' work and then waited for a response
from the student. In this way, she helped the students, in effect, to think
aloud and come up with their own proposals and suggestions. The importance of developing students' reflective skills is revisited in later lessons on
social work, hairdressing and teacher education.

What did students learn? Students' learning was very much in line with
the first definition of learning provided in Chapter 1. In this lesson, students were building on their previous experiences and practices in pro-
ducing work that reflected their individual strengths. In developing their
technical ability, they learned from the work of others but also continued
to develop their own creative ideas and visual language, exploring and
employing a diverse range of materials, techniques and ways of working.
They also learned how to give expression to the refinement of their ideas.

Lesson 8

Subject – physics
Course/level – A level
Lesson length – 90 minutes
Location – further education college
Number of students present – 12
Age – 16 to 18
Context – full-time course; 3 female and 9 male

The teacher started the lesson with a very brief introduction to what students would be doing and why, and gave them back a set of marked examination questions on wave phenomena, handed in by the students three
days prior to this lesson.

The teacher carefully guided a discussion to allow the students to come to the realization that they had successfully completed the calculations and achieved the necessary marks for that part of the examination paper but that their written explanations were not of a high enough standard. They had not explained with sufficient clarity and detail what could be concluded from results or what was being measured.

The teacher then pointed out the five short experiments that she had set out in the laboratory, each of which dealt with a different aspect of wave phenomena. She then organized the students so that they started on the experiments that would be of most value to them, given the marks they achieved on the examination paper. The activities and associated resources were highly appropriate and included a ripple tank to demonstrate interference, a CD and polarizing plastic to illustrate coherence, lenses and ray boxes to show diffraction, a ray box and a prism to demonstrate the spectrum of white light and a speaker with two sizes of plastic ball in the cone as a means of changing the frequency of sound.

At each experiment, the students were given four minutes to reflect on what was happening and to write an explanation for what they observed. When moving to the next experiment, they were asked to add to their observations or to suggest further explanations. The teacher kept time with an electronic clock on the interactive whiteboard and made sure that the students moved from one experiment to another promptly.

The students quickly understood what to do and the teacher provided timely, appropriate support for those who were initially reluctant to write anything. Some students very evidently had 'eureka moments' as it became clear to them that without putting explanations into words the examiner had no reason to award them marks, just because they had completed the relevant calculation.

After students had read out what they had written, the teacher led a very productive discussion about clarity of expression, explanations and relevant terminology. As well as making much better sense of wave phenomena, they clearly had understood the written requirements for the examination.

As indicated in her lesson plan, the teacher ensured that in the last ten minutes there was time for the students to work in pairs to review and adjust their written answers, an activity they found extremely helpful.

Commentary

What was most impressive about this lesson was the way in which the teacher, who was clearly very passionate about physics, used diagnostic assessment so effectively to advance students' learning. She devised activities to meet directly the specific needs of each of her students. Instead of taking the usual approach to revision in science subjects, whereby the teacher relies on worked examples and discussion, she went back to fundamental observation and experiments to deepen students' understanding. This is another example of the success of active learning. It also highlights the skill of this teacher, who had sufficient confidence in her knowledge of physics and of the associated pedagogy to know that this would be worth the effort and time involved.

What did these students learn? In terms of planned learning outcomes, the students found out how to get higher marks in their forthcoming examination. However, this lesson was not just about examination preparation. Improving their written work was useful in that they were developing a transferable skill. In learning more about clarity of written expression, the students discovered how much they really did, or did not, know about the topic in hand. In going back to basics on this subject, they developed a much deeper understanding of wave phenomena.

In this lesson, there was an excellent example of how a subject specialist, familiar with the structure of physics, helped a student to see how certain ideas fitted together, illustrating Bruner's sense of excitement of discovery, as discussed earlier in this chapter. At one point in the lesson, the teacher took a student aside and asked him to sketch a sine curve on paper. This he did quickly as he was familiar with this concept from his AS level mathematics studies. The teacher then asked him to sketch the same curve but with a foreshortened x-axis. Again he did so, and at that point the teacher showed him the sketch of electromagnetic radiation he had put in one of his examination paper answers. The student had not put together sine waves in mathematics and light waves in physics. The teacher had recognized this and guided him to discover the connection.

Chapter summary

Students in these four lessons were left in no doubt as to the passion and enthusiasm of their teachers. They knew that these four professionals – a chef, a classicist, an artist and a physicist – genuinely wanted them to enjoy their subjects as much as they did. Expert in both their subject and how to teach it, these teacher-practitioners commanded students' respect. They explained concepts and demonstrated techniques enthusiastically in a structured way, often enabling students to come to their own conclusions. The assessment methods they used were highly appropriate and they all demonstrated considerable expertise in questioning – the theme of the next chapter.

Lesson summary (lessons 5–8)

Table 3.1   Lesson summary (lessons 5–8)

	Particular strengths
Lesson 5 Hospitality	• Passionate and enthusiastic dual professional • High standard of students' work • Very thorough planning, with clear focus on high expectations for all students • Very well-structured demonstrations • Excellent questioning • Expert management of students and resources • Excellent formative feedback by teacher throughout lesson • Very good interweaving of equality and diversity
Lesson 6 Classical civilization	• Excellent preparation for lesson by students • High level of knowledge and mature approach to debate exhibited by students • Very knowledgeable and passionate teacher • Superb questioning by teacher • Expert management of discussion • Excellent formative feedback by teacher throughout lesson
Lesson 7 Art and design	• Highly passionate and enthusiastic teacher • High standard of students' work • Excellent planning of lesson • Industrious and inclusive atmosphere • Superb questioning • High level of constructive, formative feedback given to all students • Good promotion of cultural diversity
Lesson 8 Physics	• Excellent link in planning between activities, assessment and individual students' academic needs • Clear evidence of development of students' knowledge • Excellent resources, used very skilfully • Passionate and knowledgeable teacher • Excellent formative feedback • Very good development of students' written skills

4 Expert questioning

Assessment was discussed in Chapter 2 and the importance of formative assessment, in particular, was emphasized in terms of what makes most difference to students' learning. Questioning was identified as a prominent assessment method used by teachers of the outstanding lessons. There appears to be far more research into how and why teachers use questioning in the school sector than in either the lifelong learning sector or in higher education (Dillon 1988, 1994; Morgan and Saxton 1991; Brown and Wragg 1993). These works provide very useful tips for practitioners and the good practice they describe reflects the kind of techniques employed by teachers in the outstanding lessons in this book.

Questions that do *not* work

Before examining their practice, it might be helpful to identify what the teachers of outstanding lessons did not do. They rarely, if at all, asked meaningless rhetorical questions like 'are you with me on this?', 'do you know what you're doing?', 'shall we move on now?' or, most significantly, 'do you understand?' This last question is always a difficult one for students to answer and it provides little feedback to the teacher, who will never know, whatever the responses, whether or not students did in fact understand.

The teachers in these lessons did not answer their own questions, insult students by asking ones that were too easy, frustrate them by posing questions that were much too difficult or humiliate them with any kind of mocking or sarcastic riposte. Of course, failure to apply poor practice does not make a lesson outstanding – or even satisfactory – but it is worth pointing out that the teachers avoided these familiar traps not only because they were skilled practitioners but also because they had prepared their lessons so well and were experts in their subjects, as discussed in earlier chapters.

Questions that *do* work

Sequence and style

The approach of asking one question at a time to the whole group, pausing and then naming a particular student was evident in most of the lessons. This is, of course, preferable to stating one student's name first and then asking the question, which provides all the other students with the opportunity not to listen, let alone think about the question posed. In the numeracy class for students with learning difficulties and/or disabilities, the teacher took this approach initially but later in the lesson changed technique. She continued to ask questions to the whole group but did not allow a subsequent pause so that she could then target the question to a specific individual. This enabled her to ask differentiated questions, in terms of mathematical complexity and use of vocabulary. These varied, for example, from 'these post-it notes cost £30 and the company has charged us £45 – have we paid too much or too little?' to 'how many packets of highlighters and boxes of paper clips would we need to subtract from this list to get to that figure?'

Asking each other

Encouraging students to ask questions of each other was another feature of many of the lessons. When the human anatomy and physiology students asked the teacher questions, she redirected some of them to those students who she knew could provide the correct explanation because she had seen their written work or heard them talking about the topic. This technique worked particularly well for both the students concerned and the teacher. Those explaining had to formulate their responses carefully and it gave them the satisfaction of realizing they had indeed made sense of the given question. The recipients benefited from listening to the explanation from another student and the teacher could use the time more productively to talk or listen to other students. Race (2005) suggests that this approach of having to teach someone else something you have just learned yourself is one of the deepest learning experiences there is. When one student jokingly put his pair of spectacles in front of one of the ray boxes, the teacher took the opportunity to ask the other students if they thought the person was long-sighted or short-sighted. The teacher then asked them to justify their responses, providing another way in which she could check their understanding.

In the classical civilization lesson, the teacher was acutely aware of the different levels of understanding among his students and he very skilfully asked named individuals to explain concepts to others in the group.

Periodically in the lesson this led to debates among the students, with no intervention from the teacher. He, like the geography teacher, was particularly adept at what is known as **Socratic questioning** (Dillon 1988, 1994; Morgan and Saxton 1991; Brown and Wragg 1993), which probes evidence, tests out implications and explores alternative views.

Pauses and silence

When working with students on a one-to-one basis, the teachers asked mostly **open questions** and then allowed students time to think before responding. Neither the teacher nor the students seemed uncomfortable with pauses or silence as this scenario had clearly become established as a norm over a period of time. This approach was evident in the skills for life lesson, where the teacher sat beside each of her adult learners in turn and allowed them to take their time to respond or to find solutions for themselves, in both numeracy and literacy. It was a strong feature, too, of the art and design lesson, with the teacher making statements as well as asking questions and then waiting for students to comment. The hospitality teacher also allowed comfortable thinking time as he asked individual students questions about the methods and techniques they were using, such as 'what do you think might happen if you try this . . .?', and follow-up questions such as 'what makes you think that?'

Sensitivity

The need to avoid embarrassment was dealt with very effectively when the teacher in the human anatomy and physiology lesson in Chapter 2 undertook a recap of what her adult learners already knew about vision. By asking the learners all the same question at the same time and getting them to hold up their mini-whiteboards, she could see the responses and she used this to inform adjustments to her lesson. The learners could not easily see each other's written comments or diagrams and so were not afraid to admit how little or how much they knew.

In leading a heated debate, the geography teacher, too, was very careful not to humiliate students in front of their friends as he challenged various prejudices. He was particularly skilled at summarizing core arguments, articulating the potential implications and rephrasing what students said, with comments like 'I think what you're saying is that the views of *all* residents need to be taken into consideration if . . .' and offering the revised viewpoint to the others to consider and discuss. He also moved the debate forward on several occasions by comparing statements made by two different students and asking others in the group which they felt most represented their own views.

Inclusive whole-group discussions

In leading whole-group discussions, teachers ensured that everyone could hear students' contributions, only one person spoke at any one time and no individual student monopolized the lesson. In the physics lesson, for example, the teacher used comments such as 'That's an interesting explanation. Let's hear what the others think about it and why.' She involved students who may not have voluntarily participated at first by asking if they agreed with suggestions made by other students. **Closed questions** like this require only a one-word response but she followed this up with comments like 'tell me more . . .' or 'why do you think that . . .?' in a manner and tone that was supportive and inclusive and not in any way intimidating. In the classical civilization lesson, the teacher used non-verbal gestures and carefully worded comments to constrain one student who was very talkative.

Positive reinforcement in the form of comments such as 'well done', 'great idea', and 'brilliant answer' was used by most of the 20 teachers, but sparingly so that it was credible and genuine. The use of this type of comment as a reward is discussed further in Chapter 7 in relation to behaviourist approaches to teaching and learning.

Types and levels of question

The balance between **convergent** questions, to which there is only one right answer, and **divergent** ones, to which there might be several possible correct responses, was different in each of the lessons, depending to a certain extent on the subject matter. However, a feature all 20 lessons had in common was the significant proportion of **higher order** questions, often associated with Bloom's taxonomy (Bloom 1956). This taxonomy was described in Chapter 2, with examples of learning outcomes that relate to each level. **Lower order** questions tend to focus on the first three in the hierarchy: knowledge, comprehension and application. This usually means the questions are framed in order to check students' recall of factual information, understanding and consideration of practical relevance. The last three are analysis, synthesis and evaluation. Higher order questions at this level address students' ability to investigate, make judgements and use information to move forward in a creative way. In the school sector, much of the debate in the research (Dillon 1988, 1994; Morgan and Saxton 1991; Brown and Wragg 1993) is about the extent to which higher order questions can be used to develop pupils' thinking skills, as opposed to 'content' in the form of specified knowledge and skills. This is no less relevant in the lifelong learning sector.

Four outstanding lessons

A further four lessons are introduced in this chapter and they each reflect teachers' exemplary questioning. In the first lesson, on statistics for business studies students, the teacher very skilfully moved from quick-fire closed questions to open ones that were more demanding of the students, gradually unfolding the meaning and use of a concept the students were at first unfamiliar with. In the motor vehicle studies lesson, the teacher encouraged apprentices to question his questions and he then asked them to take on a teacher's role as they completed a practical task. The teacher of the ESOL lesson had to prepare questions very carefully, as his students had a very limited understanding of English. In the final lesson, it is the students, rather than the teacher, who asked and answered most of the questions and then peer assessed each other, as they introduced their rabbits, gerbils and hamsters.

Lesson 9

Subject – statistics
Course/level – advanced vocational business studies
Lesson length – 90 minutes
Location – further education college
Number of students present – 26
Age – 18 to 19
Context – full-time course; 8 female and 18 male

The students noisily crowded into a tiny classroom and stopped chatting as soon as the teacher, who was already in the room, raised her hand to indicate that the lesson would begin. Within seconds, the teacher launched into a series of quick-fire closed questions, directed at named individuals, about the work they had done in a previous lesson. Referring back to a task in which the students had measured their heights and plotted them on a graph, she asked questions like: Who was the tallest? Who was the shortest? If you lined up everyone in the group on the basis of height, who would be in the middle? What is the average height? How far away from the middle would Joseph be? What's the difference in height between the middle and Aleya? The teacher ensured that all students participated and she kept their attention throughout this introductory activity. The students responded well and with humour. After a few minutes of closed questions, the teacher took a different approach, with open questions to check their understanding of the terms 'mean', 'median' and 'mode'.

The teacher asked the students, in groups of two or three, to calculate the mean for three sets of data on a structured handout. Students used calculators and mobile telephones to carry out these relatively easy calculations. One of the students could not resist calling out that, although they looked different, all three sets had the same mean. This then led to a productive discussion on the limited value of the mean as a parameter. It emerged from discussion that the way data varied from the mean would also have to be considered. This was where the teacher wanted the students to go. She then introduced them to how individual datum values deviate from the mean. As a group, the students calculated the difference from the mean and the average difference from the mean for each of the datasets they had previously used. Some of the students then began to talk about the way the data deviated from the mean.

At this point, the teacher gave the concept they had begun to discuss the label of 'standard deviation' and explained that the purpose of the lesson was for them to use and apply standard deviation. She then wrote the relevant equation on the whiteboard. The meaning of 'Sigma' and 'x bar' became clear, and students could see that what at first sight looked like a difficult formula was explicable in terms of what they had just calculated. In addition, students did not at first appreciate that by squaring the difference from the mean the sign problems were eliminated. This took a little explanation, but was soon cleared up. The students then spent 15 minutes working quietly, with calculators or mobile telephones, on business-related case studies they were given on a handout. As the room was cramped and it was difficult to move around to check students' progress, the teacher remained at the front and asked specific students to check the work of others. It was clear that all students had successfully completed at least two of the tasks.

The teacher finished the lesson by thanking the students for their hard work and good humour and wishing them a good weekend.

Commentary

This was an extremely well-crafted and expertly prepared lesson. The teacher's rapid series of closed questions at the start of the lesson was theatrical to a certain extent and partly implemented in order to gain control of what could easily have been a disruptive group of students. As students on an applied business studies course, they were not all highly motivated in relation to learning mathematics or statistics. However, as is the case in other lessons in this book, the teacher's approach, enthusiasm and passion clearly had a positive impact on them and their desire to learn. The lower order, closed questions did have a purpose in addition to helping with behaviour management. The reminder about the distribution of their heights fed neatly into later higher order questions and activities and the checking of students' understanding of key statistical terms, before moving on to the main part, and purpose, of the lesson.

What did these students learn? Firstly, the students learned the *meaning* of 'standard deviation'. They were able to describe this concept accurately in their own words and apply it to business-related examples. In terms of their learning, this reflected a significant change in knowledge and understanding. Secondly, they learned how to *calculate* standard deviation. These two stages were possible because, demonstrating expertise in both her subject and in pedagogy, the teacher provided the appropriate type and level of scaffolding for students throughout the lesson.

This lesson provides a good example of when the introduction to the aim of a lesson is best left to midway through for maximum effect, and best explained in plain English. Had this teacher begun this lesson, with 26 lively young people, stating that 'today's topic is standard deviation and by the end of the lesson you will have undertaken at least one calculation . . .' she would probably not have gained their attention, let alone interest.

This teacher demonstrated excellent classroom management skills. This aspect of teaching is explored further in Chapter 5. The lesson is also an example of how teachers deal creatively with events if things do not go to plan. A discussion with her after the lesson revealed that she had been very frustrated at having to change rooms and the fact that she did not have access to an interactive whiteboard. She had planned to use it to display and manipulate graphs, as well as the equation and the tasks. With no space available to walk around and behind students, she could not check their written work but addressed this successfully by nominating specific students to check the work of others. She did not share this frustration with the students.

Lesson 10

Subject – motor vehicle studies
Course/level – intermediate
Lesson length – three hours
Location – work-based learning provider
Number of students present – eight
Age – 16 to 24
Context – full-time course; 1 female and 7 male

As the apprentices arrived at the workshop, the teacher checked they each had the appropriate protective clothing, shoes and safety glasses.

The teacher started promptly, explaining to the apprentices that they would be learning how to replace a carburettor. He gathered the students around a large screen in one corner of the workshop then showed a presentation of the process, pausing the video clip after each stage to ask questions like 'Why do we need to check the old carburettor against the new one?',

'Why do you think the mechanic checked the throttle bore?', 'What might carbon in the throttle bore indicate?', 'Why use a strong solvent to clean the area where you mount the new carburettor?', 'What might happen if you don't?' In addition to seeking answers from students, he also asked them why they thought he had asked specific questions. Their responses gave him a clear idea as to the level of their understanding and problem-solving skills.

Once they had viewed the presentation, the teacher gave them a hand-out summarizing what had been covered and explained that they would work in pairs on each of the four cars. One student would replace the car-burettor and the other would observe and take on the role of teacher, asking questions to check their partner's knowledge as they complete each stage of the process. They would then swap roles and repeat the process.

The teacher suggested they work with someone they had not been paired with recently and the apprentices sorted this out among themselves speedily and with good humour. They were much more concerned about being the observer/teacher than the mechanic, but they undertook both roles very seriously and competently. The teacher observed them at work but kept a low profile during this part of the lesson, only occasionally con-tributing suggestions or responding to questions.

When they had completed the activity he asked students to peer assess one another and to fill in the assessment grid for their partner. Students were comfortable with this approach, having worked in this way in previous lessons. The teacher kept a watchful eye on this assessment and provided support where necessary.

The lesson ended with a quick summary of what they had learned and an indication of what they would be doing in the following lesson.

Commentary

The teacher in this lesson demonstrated considerable expertise in question-ing. Encouraging the apprentices to think about *why* he asked them certain questions proved to be a powerful assessment strategy and it successfully promoted the kind of higher order thinking referred to earlier in relation to Bloom's taxonomy.

What did these students learn? These apprentices were not simply going through the motions of changing a carburettor. They did, indeed, acquire the technical skills to perform this task and demonstrate the required level of competence. However, they also gained a considerable amount of asso-ciated technical knowledge. Problem-solving, collaborative-working and peer assessment skills were also developed very effectively, made possible by the teacher's approach and his management of the lesson.

Assessment was not simply about ticking off competences on a check-list, although this was done at the end of the lesson. Getting students to observe each other, ask questions, take on the teacher's role and then assess their peers all served to provide both the teacher and the students with plenty of evidence as to the knowledge they had acquired to underpin the way in which they had applied their understanding. As noted by Race (2005), peer assessment of this kind can be very valuable. It was evident, for example, that the apprentices deepened their learning by applying assessment criteria to the work of their peers.

In noting what an experienced mechanic might do in specific situations, the teacher alternated between the pronouns 'he' and 'she'. This modelling had the desired effect in that students used the same pronouns in their responses. At no point did he or any of the students make reference to the fact that one of the students was female and the atmosphere in the workshop was at all times professional and inclusive.

Lesson 11

Subject – English for speakers of other languages (ESOL)
Course/level – entry
Lesson length – one hour
Location – further education college
Number of students present – eight
Age – adults
Context – full-time course; all from Afghanistan and all male

This lesson took place early on in the academic year and the teacher had had only one other lesson with this group. This was a one-hour tutorial and the college had a strict policy that all teachers, including those teaching ESOL, had to cover the same tutorial syllabus and use standard material wherever possible.

The teacher got the learners settled quickly, directing them to sit at the front of the classroom, using gestures in addition to instructions in English. To gain silence, he raised his index finger to his lips and looked directly at individuals. When they stopped talking, he smiled and gave a nod and a 'thumbs up'.

Very skilfully, the teacher ensured that the learners became familiar with their timetables by making them practise the pronunciation of days of the week, times and teachers' names. He asked learners carefully prepared questions to check their interpretation of the information he had given them. The responses confirmed that learners were using their newly acquired vocabulary correctly and that they knew where they had to be on each day and at what time. As is the case for many ESOL teachers, he used realia, such as calendars, a map of the college, clocks and mobile telephones, to good effect. It was a very lively session and the teacher had to repeatedly make the silence gesture to stop the learners all talking at once.

Once they were confident about their timetable, he moved on to the college newsletter. He gave them each a copy to keep but also displayed an electronic version on the interactive whiteboard for them to look at as he indicated the three items they needed to understand, which he had highlighted. The first one was term dates for the year and the teacher encouraged the learners to put these into their diaries. For three of the eight learners, this meant entering the dates into their mobile telephones, which the teacher encouraged them to do.

The second item was the telephone number to ring if they were going to be late or absent. Again, learners put the number in their own telephones and then undertook a role play in pairs, ensuring that they were able to say their name and the fact that they would not attend the college that day. After this, the teacher pointed to a notice on the wall which showed a picture of a mobile telephone with a red line through it. The learners laughed and the teacher explained that during lessons they were not allowed to receive or make calls.

The third item was notification of a forthcoming 'international' party at the college. To help them appreciate what this might involve, the teacher showed them a short video clip of last year's party, with male and female learners of all nationalities clearly enjoying themselves. It was carefully edited to blur students' faces. The video clip caused much laughter and amusement.

Commentary

As with any language class, particularly where the learners are relative beginners, the teacher of this lesson needed to be very precise when asking questions. His accompanying tone, facial expressions and emphasis on specific words all helped learners to listen, repeat and practise with confidence.

What did these students learn? In line with the planned outcomes for this lesson, they learned the meaning and pronunciation of 'survival' vocabulary that would be of immediate use to them. They also learned more about the college and its values. In terms of attitudes, they learned that all talking at once was not deemed to be acceptable behaviour.

The teacher's clear understanding of the structure of English, and of the associated pedagogy, enabled him to know which questions to ask, in which order and when to introduce new vocabulary. As discussed in Chapter 3, all subject areas have their own structures that experts are familiar with and learners need to learn, so that they can see the patterns and make the relevant connections.

With languages, for example, students learn, either **deductively** by being told or **inductively** by discovery, the rules about tenses and how to conjugate a verb. They demonstrate their understanding of structures by

applying it to new situations or vocabulary. Indeed, even in this beginners' lesson, there was evidence of the application of one such rule by one of the learners. Having initially said 'three day', he corrected himself quickly and said 'three days' because he remembered that plural words usually end with 's'. Without understanding this pattern, students would need to learn a plural version of every single new noun they encountered.

Sensitive to the fact that this group of learners all had the same first language and were all male, the teacher had thought about how he could reflect the diversity of the college and the fact that this was something that was celebrated. He chose, therefore, to select a video showing both male and female students of differing ages and backgrounds.

Lesson 12

Subject – animal care
Course/level – intermediate
Lesson length – two hours
Location – further education college
Number of students present – ten
Age – 16 to 18
Context – full-time course; all female

The students were undertaking a course to prepare them to work as assistants in veterinary care or in establishments where small animals are cared for.

The teacher did not need to do much in the way of introduction to the lesson, as the students knew exactly what they had to do. She reminded them briefly that they would all learn more about the care of small animals, as well as develop their presentation skills. She pointed to the code of conduct on the wall that they had agreed in the previous lesson and she also checked they had their notes and, most importantly, their live animal. She then told them authoritatively the order in which they would give their presentation, thereby avoiding any requests for a change in sequence and possible delays.

With eight minutes allocated for each presentation, the teacher was keen to get started. She set the countdown timer on the interactive whiteboard and each student took it in turn, accompanied by a variety of rabbits, gerbils and hamsters, to give a presentation on the care of their chosen animal, based on the research they had each undertaken in preparation for this lesson. This included information about cleaning, feeding, handling and administering basic medical care, as well as a brief examination and discussion of health and safety issues. Although a few of the students were nervous, the standard of presentation was high, primarily because they had done more than enough research. This was evident from the confidence with which they answered questions from their peers. Students' questioning of each other was mature and thoughtful.

The students were given two or three minutes in silence after each presentation to complete a peer evaluation form, highlighting three aspects they found particularly useful from the presentation and one that could have been improved. These were then passed directly to the teacher.

The teacher listened carefully to the students, making structured notes under different headings on the interactive whiteboard. She kept the proceedings strictly to time, with some difficulty on a few occasions, as students would have happily overrun. This was mostly due to follow-up questions by other students rather than poor planning of the presentations.

After the final presentation, the teacher gave students the completed evaluation forms from their peers, which they read quietly for a few minutes. She then used the notes on the whiteboard as the focus for a summary of what had been learned, followed by a whole-group discussion. She started with a few closed questions, checking some basic facts that had been presented, and then moved on to more exploratory questions, such as 'So, why do you assume that . . .', 'Do you think this might be the same for other animals? If so, why and which ones?'

Students spent the last few minutes clearing up the room and the teacher reminded them that the homework was to write up a one-page self-evaluation of their presentation, taking into account the feedback from their peers. The template she gave them also required students to comment on the questions they had asked their peers.

Commentary

There are many advantages to encouraging students to ask each other questions (Dillon 1988). In this lesson, it shifted the focus away from the teacher for most of the time and made the students feel responsible for the pace and flow of the lesson. They listened attentively to each other, participated with sensible contributions and developed their own questioning skills. They were able to do this so well largely because the teacher had prepared them for this task in the previous lesson. Guided by her, the students had agreed a code of conduct that included their own suggestions, such as keeping to time, not all talking at once, being polite and neither dominating nor remaining silent. Having also discussed different types of question, the students demonstrated what they had learned by asking a mixture of open and closed questions, as well as several follow-up and probing ones, the responses to which highlighted the extensive research students had undertaken.

In the few cases where students' responses were not as detailed or clear as they could have been, the teacher incorporated this into her notes on the whiteboard and covered the relevant topic in the group discussion. Her questioning was sensitive and positive in focusing on some of the best contributions, while also addressing any misunderstanding.

What did these students learn? These students extended their factual knowledge about the care of small animals, quite considerably in many cases. They also developed their skills in research, preparing and delivering presentations, asking and responding to questions and peer assessment.

As in the motor vehicle studies lesson, the advantages of peer assessment, as outlined by Race (2005), were evident in this lesson. The students in this lesson received more feedback than the teacher would have been able to give them. Some of the students seemed to find it easier and more enjoyable to take feedback from a fellow student than from the teacher. In a few cases, they took advantage of observing what other students did particularly well and took a similar approach. Where they noted practice that was not so good, they avoided doing the same. For example, when one of the students agreed to take questions before the end of her presentation, she got sidetracked and left out some important material she had intended to talk about. Noting this, the next student announced at the start of her presentation that she would only take questions when she had finished her input.

The self-assessment task for homework would provide the students with a further opportunity to deepen their learning and develop their reflective skills.

Chapter summary

These four lessons demonstrate the gains to be made when teachers take time to think in advance about the questions they will ask in a lesson. This is particularly important when question and answer is the main method of assessment, as it is so often. When questions, or a framework for types of question, are planned beforehand it can aid the flow and pace of the lesson, check the appropriate levels of understanding and contribute to maintaining students' motivation and interest. It also minimizes the risk of asking the type of meaningless rhetorical questions described earlier in this chapter. Of course, not all questions can or should be planned in advance, as teachers need to be able to respond freely to changing dynamics in a lesson. It is tempting, though, particularly for experienced teachers, to assume that *all* questioning can be done 'on the hoof'. The teachers of outstanding lessons successfully encouraged students to ask as well as answer questions. These teachers were also adept at varying the level of their questions to ensure that they were making students think, analyse and reflect as well as simply recall information.

Lesson summary (lessons 9–12)

Table 4.1   Lesson summary (lessons 9–12)

	Particular strengths
Lesson 9 Statistics	• Excellent planning • Clear evidence of students applying newly acquired knowledge and skills • Exemplary questioning by teacher • Excellent classroom management skills, successfully preventing potential disruption • Very good formative assessment, enabling teacher and students to judge level of understanding throughout lesson
Lesson 10 Motor vehicle studies	• Very well-planned lesson • Successful completion of tasks by all apprentices • Superb questioning by teacher • Excellent feedback from teacher and peers • Good development of apprentices' questioning and thinking skills • Excellent use of peer assessment, helping apprentices to understand assessment criteria • Good practice modelled by teacher in relation to equality and diversity
Lesson 11 ESOL	• Meticulously planned lesson • Highly relevant knowledge and skills acquired by learners • Excellent feedback by teacher throughout lesson • Excellent questioning by teacher • Very well-designed tasks linked to learners' ability and institutional requirements • Very good link to promotion of diversity
Lesson 12 Animal care	• High standard of students' presentations • Mature questioning by students • Highly appropriate resources • Very good planning by teacher, following on from previous lesson • Very good management of lesson by teacher • Excellent use of peer assessment • Excellent development of students' research skills • Excellent development of students' presentation skills

5 High expectations

Students might enjoy activities and discussions and report favourably on the passion and enthusiasm of their teacher but this does not necessarily mean that they have learned anything or as much as they could have learned. Observers with a lesson observation checklist may positively confirm a series of features that are necessary for a satisfactory, good or outstanding lesson, without giving an appropriate weighting to each of them or making an overall 'common sense' judgement. One such feature commonly listed is 'student engagement'. Students may well be 'fully engaged' but what does that actually mean? It usually means that they are busy doing something. They may well be busy, but what they are doing may not be sufficiently challenging, or possibly even relevant. Similarly, some observers note that 'learning took place' without specifying *what* learning, at what level or how they know.

A common characteristic of all 20 outstanding lessons was the high expectations teachers had of their students and this was reflected in the excellent standard of students' work in the form of what they did, said or produced.

High expectations are important because, as noted by Ramsden (2003: 62), students adapt to the requirements they perceive teachers to make of them. Generally, students try to please their teachers and will do what they think will bring rewards. In their planning, teaching and assessment, teachers of the outstanding lessons were ambitious, rather than safe. This meant that their students knew that they were expected to be ambitious, too. The two science teachers set high standards and enabled every single student in their lessons to apply their understanding through well-devised activities. In the numeracy lesson, the teacher ensured that everyone completed challenging mathematical tasks successfully, whatever the student's level, learning difficulty or disability. The hospitality teacher was confident he could get students to prepare a much higher than usual number of covers, all to a professional standard. The geography teacher took his students beyond syllabus requirements, as did the motor vehicle studies teacher, who wanted to be certain that apprentices knew precisely what they were doing and why.

However ambitious a teacher is, the students must either need or want to learn for the lesson to be successful. The extent to which excellent teaching can in itself motivate students has been alluded to in previous chapters and will be discussed more fully now.

Motivation

Much has been written about motivation by psychologists, business and human resource specialists as well as educationalists. Three of the many models have been selected here in an attempt to gain insight into students' motivation in the outstanding lessons. The first is Race's ripple model (2005), the second is what is known as expectancy theory (Feather 1982) and the third is theory X and theory Y (McGregor 1966).

Race's ripple model

Two of the five factors underpinning successful learning identified by Race (2005) relate to motivation: *wanting* to learn and *needing* to learn. He argues that these factors, along with *learning by doing*, *learning through feedback* and *digesting*, are like ripples on a pond, in that they all affect one another and occur more or less simultaneously. The last three factors have been important features of the 12 lessons described thus far and are also present in the next eight. It is helpful, therefore, to reflect on how the first two apply to the students in the same lessons.

There was no evidence in any of the lessons of a lack of motivation by students. One could argue that this is related to the methodological approach taken and that, had students been disengaged, the lessons would not have been judged outstanding. Indeed, it is the case that many of the students *needed* to learn. The reasons why the skills for life adults were keen to learn were explained in Chapter 2, reflecting a desire to help their children and/or improve their job prospects. For the newly arrived adult learners from Afghanistan in the ESOL lesson, the acquisition of English was essential to enable them to function in the United Kingdom. The art and design students were focused on securing a place in higher education, as were most of the students studying geography, physics and classical civilization. Clearly, the direct link between the need to learn and employment was most evident in the hospitality, animal care and motor vehicle studies lessons.

Race's ripple model is useful in explaining what happened in the outstanding lessons in that, even if the students' motivation was initially purely extrinsic (*needing to learn*), the teachers were highly successful in creating an environment that enabled students to enjoy a variety of activities, tasks and discussions (*learning by doing*), make sense of what they had learned (*digesting*) and benefit from feedback from the teacher and, in some cases, from other students (*learning through feedback*). Teachers were careful to emphasize the knowledge and skills students would gain rather than simply the need to meet formal assessment requirements. Even in the physics revision lesson, which was based to some extent on examination technique, there was also a focus on deepening understanding. All these strategies appear to have given many, if not most, of the students a desire to learn further (*wanting to learn*). There may be some truth in the well-known cliché that success breeds success.

Expectancy theory

The expectancy theory asserts that in order to be motivated people have to have both the *desire* for the outcome and the *expectancy* that they can obtain that goal (Harper 1997). If students believe that a particular behaviour will lead to a particular outcome but they place no value on that outcome, they will not be motivated. Similarly, if they place a high value on the goal but have convinced themselves they are unlikely to achieve it, then again they will not be motivated.

In the 20 outstanding lessons, students did appear to recognize the importance of the 'outcome' in the form of a qualification and/or improved employment prospects. The extent to which they valued learning for its own sake was impossible to measure, but many of them seemed to relish the camaraderie, discussions and activities and they clearly enjoyed the sense of achievement on successful completion of a task. The fact that the teachers gave regular feedback and assured them that they *would* be successful was important in terms of motivation, in light of this model. It provided them with the 'expectancy' that they would obtain the outcome they desired. A significant proportion of the students in the 20 outstanding lessons had failed in the past to gain important knowledge, skills and qualifications. This was particularly the case for those in the skills for life lesson and, as will be evident in Chapters 5 and 6, it is also pertinent to the students in the bricklaying and cleaning and support services lessons. Had these students been led to believe that they were likely to be unsuccessful yet again, they would not have been as motivated and so the cycle of failure would continue.

Theory X and theory Y

In creating this type of positive and inclusive classroom climate and assuring students that they would be successful, teachers were operating according to McGregor's theory Y (1966). They were assuming that students would work without coercion and that they could exercise self-direction and have the potential for creative work. Although McGregor's work is about assumptions managers make about their employees, it is as applicable to teachers and students.

Elements of both X and Y are likely to exist in most lessons, but teachers who have more of a theory X approach assume that students do not want to learn, are lazy and reluctant to assume responsibility. These teachers usually take a deficit view of their students. They are most likely to blame the students if lessons do not go to plan or suggest that the reason is that students are not as bright or as keen as they used to be. When teachers make these theory X assumptions, the problem, as highlighted by Biggs (1999), is that they and their students can become anxious and cynical. When this happens, students are more like to take a surface approach to their learning.

Andragogy

There is an argument that adult learners, who make the choice to attend lessons, will inevitably be more motivated than younger students. The andragogical model has for many decades been the central model of adult learning. Andragogy, mentioned in the first chapter, is most widely associated with the influential work of Malcolm Knowles. Knowles (1980) compares assumptions of pedagogy and andragogy. He suggests that pedagogy assumes the role of the student is a dependent one. Andragogy, by way of contrast, assumes that adults are self-directing. Pedagogy sees students' prior experience as of little value to the teacher, whereas andragogy recognizes and builds on adults' wealth of experience. Knowles distinguishes, too, between the readiness to learn of younger students and of adult learners. He suggests that the former learn when an external authority, such as a parent, school or college, tells them to do so, whereas adults are ready to learn something when they experience a need to learn it in order to cope with real-life problems. Pedagogy, he asserts, focuses on subject content, whereas andragogy is more problem centred.

In the seven outstanding lessons involving adult learners, the teachers taught in a way that acknowledged the principles of andragogy. It was clearly the case that the learners were motivated because they were at a stage in their lives where they needed to learn. The teachers did indeed very effectively tap into learners' life experiences as a rich resource on which to draw. This was evident in the human anatomy and physiology, skills for life and ESOL lessons. Further examples are provided in this chapter in the social work lesson and in Chapter 6 with the information technology, teacher education and family learning lessons. Less effective teaching, though, may well have returned some of the adults in these lessons to the cycle of failure as discussed above in relation to expectancy theory. Many of the teaching methods used with adults were also applied to younger students, suggesting that pedagogy and andragogy may not be as mutually exclusive as implied earlier. This will be explored further in Chapter 7.

Whether the students were young or older, if the lessons had been less stimulating, those who were not highly motivated may well have 'switched off' or become disruptive. This did not happen because the lessons were extremely well planned to avoid this scenario and the teachers were very proficient practitioners who employed subtle and highly effective class-room management techniques.

Classroom management

The fact that no students were disruptive in any of the 20 lessons does not mean that these teachers were lucky in getting highly self-motivated students. Instead, it reflects the fact that, through their planning and practice, the teachers were sufficiently skilful to *prevent* disruption.

Much of the research into classroom management in schools is relevant to the lifelong learning sector. It is clear, for example, that the four rules of classroom management devised by Smith and Laslett (2001) had been applied in the 20 lessons in this book. Their seemingly simplistic rules are: get them in; get them out; get on with it; and get on with them. The first rule is about the importance of a brisk start to lessons. The teachers of the outstanding lessons all started promptly and smoothly, setting a clear tone for the rest of the lesson. They did not allow themselves to be sidetracked by the arrival of latecomers, the setting up of resources or activities or any other distractions. They ensured that students were seated quickly and that as little time as possible was lost before starting the lesson. The second rule relates to the way in which teachers conclude lessons. Although in several of the lessons students were reluctant to leave, there was no sense of teachers or students running out of time or of lessons finishing abruptly or inconclusively. All 20 lessons ended on a positive note, often with a summary of what had been achieved, an indication of what would be covered in the next lesson and the teacher thanking students for their contribution.

In the third rule – get on with it – the 'it' refers to the main content of the lesson. Smith and Laslett (2001) suggest that problems with behaviour often arise out of a mismatch between the content of the lesson and students' ability and Huxley (2001) makes this same observation specifically about the further education sector. As discussed in earlier chapters, the 20 teachers in this book planned their lessons extremely well to get the balance right and to ensure that activities were neither too easy nor too difficult. By keeping the students busy and meaningfully engaged in suitably challenging and interesting activities, behaviour problems were minimized. The final rule is about the way in which effective teachers develop good personal relationships with their students by fostering mutual respect and trust. Indeed, the strong rapport between teachers and their students was a striking feature of all the lessons in this book.

Jacob Kounin's work, although written in the 1970s and similarly focused on school pupils, is also very helpful in gaining an insight into what the teachers of the outstanding lessons in this book did so well. Often, the techniques they used were so subtle that they could have easily been missed by inexperienced observers. For example, each teacher demonstrated what Kounin called *with-it-ness*, which describes the way in which highly effective teachers know exactly what is going on in their classroom at all times. They routinely made eye contact with students, used their names when speaking to students and established an atmosphere of strong mutual respect, even in the case of the ESOL lesson, which was only the second time the teacher had met the group. Kounin's research (1977) suggests that when the students know that their teacher is *with-it* they are less likely to misbehave. This seems to apply as much to the adult learners as to the younger students. The ESOL learners, for example, would have happily chatted to each other in their own language for the duration of the lesson, had the teacher not been so skilled in maintaining their attention. The human anatomy and physiology learners may have wandered 'off task' had their teacher not maintained a careful eye on what was happening in those lessons.

With the younger students, the teachers were particularly good at applying what Kounin called *overlapping* – the ability to deal with two issues at the same time. In both the geography and statistics lessons, for example, there were occasions when, in the midst of talking to one individual, the teachers spotted another student in the room who had either finished a task or who looked as if she or he might be disruptive. In most cases, making eye contact or using some other kind of appropriate non-verbal gesture was sufficient to get these students back on track. On the one occasion when this did not work, the teacher simply asked the individual a closed question and this had the desired effect.

The lessons demonstrated the skill with which the teachers managed transitions, which also features in Kounin's research. Teachers moved students smoothly from one activity to another, avoiding a lull in momentum and the potential loss of focus. This was particularly well done in the statistics lesson, where the teacher had 26 lively young students who might easily have become distracted. All the teachers maintained the pace and flow of their lessons extremely well. In both the physics and animal care lessons, for example, the teachers used electronic timers to keep students to the required deadlines. Sophisticated questioning techniques, as discussed in Chapter 4, also contributed to maintaining momentum and minimizing disruption.

Four outstanding lessons

The high expectations teachers had of their students are reflected in different ways in each of the four lessons that feature in this chapter. In the lesson on media studies, the teacher encouraged his students to produce computer-based work of the highest possible standard by emphasizing how demanding their clients would be once the students started working in this field and by drawing on his own background prior to being a teacher. In the social work lesson, the teacher subtly used probing questions and pauses to encourage her students to reflect on their placement in a way that genuinely helped them to identify their own areas for development. Work of a professional standard was critical in the hairdressing salon, with the teacher demanding high standards of her students as they undertook treatments with real clients. Finally, in the cleaning and support services lesson, based in a young offenders' institution, the teacher managed to instil in the students, who needed to seek employment on release, a sense of pride in their work.

Lesson 13

Subject – media studies
Course/level – advanced
Lesson length – 90 minutes
Location – further education college
Number of students present – eight
Age – 16 to 18
Context – full-time course; 6 male and 2 female

Students arrived early and went directly to their computers. By the time the teacher arrived, the students had all started work on an assignment that involved designing a website. The quietly spoken teacher got their attention for just a few moments to announce his arrival and to confirm that students would continue working on their assignment, which was based on a real client brief.

The students were extremely industrious. For the most part, they worked quietly on their own, but occasionally one student would ask another a question and they helped each other out. This was done in a friendly but businesslike manner and never drifted into chat or disruptive behaviour.

Without disturbing the rest of the group, the teacher sat next to each student in turn to find out what stage they were at and to provide academic, design and technical support where necessary. He also encouraged several students to use the spelling and grammar-checking facilities on their computer more carefully to avoid errors, pointing out examples where they could not rely on the technology. He drew very effectively on his own professional experience in both the private and charity sectors to respond to students' questions about content, style, language and layout. He skilfully encouraged each student to produce work of a professional standard, praising them for what they had done well but also directing them to 'go the extra mile'. He did not relate this to getting higher marks for their assignment, but focused instead on the benefits to students of developing their skills further and learning more about the application, as well as the need to meet – and indeed exceed – clients' expectations when working in a commercial environment.

In the last five minutes of the lesson, students walked around the room and looked at each other's work displayed on the computer screens. They were complimentary about the standard of work, as was the teacher. He asked the students if they would be able to finish this part of the assignment before the next lesson and they all readily confirmed that this would not be a problem.

Commentary

There was an almost palpable buzz of excitement in the room as the students explored the application they were using and discovered its different features. The standard of their work was very high and the students responded well to the teacher's constructive feedback and suggestions that they continue to improve what they had done, rather than simply meet the minimum assessment requirements. The students were all highly motivated and clearly wanted to learn, so much so that they were still discussing their websites with each other as they walked out of the lesson and they were making plans to go to the learning resources centre later that day to continue with this project.

What did these students learn? They extended their knowledge and their technical and design skills significantly in relation to the application they were using and in this industrious atmosphere they also learned how to work and learn independently and how to solve problems. Through research and analysis of the client brief, they learned more about the nature, context and values of the relevant industry.

Like the classical civilization lesson in Chapter 3, this lesson demonstrates that a traditional lesson format, be it 'chalk and talk' or having students sitting at a computer for the duration of the lesson, can be highly successful if planned well, with meaningful tasks, ongoing formative assessment and high-quality feedback from the teacher. A regular change of activity, for the sake of it, is not always necessary.

Lesson 14

Subject – social work
Course/level – access to higher education
Lesson length – 90 minutes
Location – further education college
Number of students present – 13
Age – adults
Context – full-time course; all female

The learners had just completed a work placement and this was the first time they were back together as a group at the college. Most were already assembled in the room some ten minutes before the lesson was scheduled to begin and they chatted to one another enthusiastically. One learner arrived 15 minutes after the lesson had started due to a medical appointment, but she had already alerted the teacher to this.

Sitting in a circle, the teacher spent five minutes welcoming the learners back to the college and explaining that she hoped they would be able to share their experiences of their work placements, note what they had learned and plan any future actions to improve their performance. She highlighted the six headings she had written on the flip chart: description, feelings, evaluation, analysis, conclusion and action. She then suggested that learners might wish to follow that format but that it was in no way compulsory.

The teacher then asked one of the learners to start. She had chosen this articulate person to speak first as she was confident that this learner would set a good example for the others to follow. As the learner spoke, the others were very respectful and listened intently. The teacher asked a few follow-up questions and then sat quietly while other learners asked questions, gave suggestions on how they would have dealt with the clients or related experiences of their own that were similar.

The teacher wrote on the whiteboard unobtrusively while the learners talked, capturing points agreed by the learners or ones she felt were important. When the discussion had reached a natural end with one learner, the teacher gave a nod and smile to another learner as an indication that the group was ready for the next speaker. The learners had been informed, prior to their placements, that they would have to give this presentation and they were clearly well prepared. Occasionally, the teacher asked a learner to expand a point she was making or asked another learner what she might have done in that situation. One learner raised a concern about perceptions of racist attitudes by a colleague at her placement. The other learners provided constructive, practical advice and comments and also made helpful references to institutional policies on equality and diversity.

All the learners were actively involved in the discussions and it was clear from the animated way they spoke that they had all valued their work placements and were benefiting further from talking and hearing about the others.

After approximately an hour, the teacher brought the discussion to an end and she reviewed the notes on the whiteboard, relating common threads back to the work they had completed during the year and further topics to come. The learners then worked alone for ten minutes, developing an action plan for their reflective journal, articulating areas for development arising from the experience. The teacher asked for these to be given in at the next session.

Commentary

As with the geography, classical civilization and media studies lessons, this was fairly traditional in terms of teaching methods and there were no additional learning resources. The highly experienced teacher facilitated the lesson in a very sensitive and effective way, helping these adult learners to develop their reflective skills. She had created an atmosphere in which they felt comfortable talking honestly and openly about their experiences on placement. They were relieved to discover that the difficulties they had experienced were not unique to them and they valued the opportunity to hear how others had approached similar situations. They recognized that they could use an action plan as a relevant and realistic way for them to identify how to undertake their social work practice more effectively in the future. The teacher did not intervene in the discussion about racist attitudes as she felt the learners had covered this issue themselves adequately and very effectively.

What did these students learn? The first definition of learning in Chapter 1 is pertinent here. Reflection of the kind undertaken in this lesson is a key part of experiential learning. Facilitated by the teacher, these adults were turning their experience into learning (Boud et al. 1985). With the support of their peers, they were drawing on that experience to understand their practice, frame problems and suggest actions. This in turn would lead them, at a later stage, to reflect on the consequences of those actions. As an experienced social worker herself, the teacher was also inducting learners into the relevant **community of practice** by placing emphasis on reflection as a skill the learners would need for their profession. There is a convincing argument that professionals learn their skills through practising them in new situations and through reflection rather than the mechanistic application of theory (Schön 1982). This relates as much to teachers in the lifelong learning sector as it does in this case to trainee social workers.

Lesson 15

Subject – hairdressing
Course/level – intermediate and advanced
Lesson length – two hours
Location – further education college
Age – 16 to 18
Number of students present – 15
Context – full-time course; all female

This brisk and challenging session took place in the college's salon. The teacher started the lesson by eliciting from students relevant health and safety information, the essentials of good client care and the importance of working to commercial times and standards. She allocated clients according to each student's level. The students set up their workstations speedily and collected their clients from the reception area.

The students undertook well-focused consultations to identify their clients' suitability for chemical treatments or requirements for styling or blow-drying. They communicated clearly and in a friendly manner and, where appropriate, used style books, colour charts and images very effectively to initiate, support or counter clients' suggestions.

As part of the pre-treatment consultations, students performed tests on clients' hair correctly and with confidence, demonstrating their ability to apply theory they had learned to practice. In several cases, this involved testing chemicals to colour, curl or relax the hair. Students interpreted all of the test outcomes correctly and these were checked carefully by the teacher.

The teacher circulated and prioritized support for those students giving chemical treatments. She questioned them skilfully about the outcomes of the consultation, planned treatment and subsequent products and processes, before giving them approval to proceed. With considerable skill and sensitivity so as not to undermine students in front of their clients, the teacher asked students carefully worded questions and encouraged them to suggest adjustments to treatment plans where appropriate. The students recognized the subtlety of this approach, appreciated the subtext and responded in a professional and mature manner.

The teacher gradually withdrew direct support as students worked confidently and competently with clients. She observed each student carefully and, in interacting with the clients, she modelled the kind of communication and care she demanded of her students. In this well-ordered and productive learning environment, the students demonstrated a range of excellent practical skills, for example in applying colour, shampooing hair and weaving highlights.

When finished with their clients, the students took a serious approach to an analysis of the standard of their work, based on self-assessment, feedback from the teacher and comments from the clients. Their evaluations were constructively critical and not overly descriptive. They used this to inform action plans and targets to improve their existing skills and develop new ones. While they undertook this task on a computer, the teacher circulated, listening to students, answering their questions and providing support where appropriate.

Commentary

This lesson, as with the hospitality and motor vehicle lessons, highlights the key role of dual professionals, expert in both their vocational area and in teaching.

What did these students learn? Each student improved her technical skills. In addition, the students acquired the kind of tacit knowledge associated with this workplace environment, as discussed in Chapter 3. As with the hospitality lesson, this lesson provides an example of 'situated learning' (Lave and Wenger 1991), in that the students' learning took place in the same context in which it was applied, and this was integral to the way in which they worked. Students learned how to become 'insiders' so that they felt comfortable identifying with this particular community, speaking its language and behaving as a member.

The high quality of the students' evaluation of their own work demonstrated the way in which the teacher had created a climate whereby students felt comfortable with reflection as a means to improve practice.

Given their experience of being taught for several months by this authoritative but friendly teacher, the students were under no illusions in this lesson about the high standards expected of them. The assessment of their practice was more than simply checking minimum competence levels. Students took great pride in their work and were keen to demonstrate both to the teacher and to their clients their developing expertise. Directive at the start of the lesson, the teacher adapted her approach as the lesson progressed and by the second half she was listening and observing rather than talking. This reflects the type of *fading* discussed in Chapter 3 in relation to the cognitive apprenticeship model.

The students' high level of motivation was most probably linked initially to their *need to learn*, as discussed earlier, in order to work in the profession of their choice. However, the teacher's passion, enthusiasm and desire for the students to work to the highest possible standard clearly also had an impact on their motivation. Like all the other teachers of the outstanding lessons, she demonstrated the theory Y assumptions about her students and they responded accordingly.

Lesson 16

Subject – cleaning and support services
Course/level – entry and intermediate
Lesson length – 90 minutes
Location – young offenders' institution
Number of students present – eight
Age – 16 to 18
Context – full-time course; all male

This expertly taught practical lesson on floor cleaning was for students who needed to gain the skills and an associated qualification to improve their employment prospects on release from a young offenders' institution.

The teacher had prepared the area for the demonstration of mopping and cleaning a vinyl-covered floor and had all the materials ready for the demonstration. She reminded students about the ground rules they had established in an earlier lesson and then asked a series of questions about health and safety, which the students answered correctly. The students watched the teacher's demonstration attentively and listened carefully to her commentary. Aware of the low literacy level of most of the students, she provided a very clear handout, with diagrams and pictures, explaining the steps involved in the demonstration. She referred to the handout throughout the lesson, highlighting difficult or unusual spellings or words where appropriate.

The teacher very deftly steered the students through the process of learning this practical skill and used the task to instil in them a sense of pride in doing a job to a high standard. She was enthusiastic and in charge of where the lesson would go. The students appeared to trust her to take them somewhere worth going. Her verbal register and modes of address with students were authoritative but lightly familiar, although she modified her tone as and when required to chivvy, coax, encourage, praise, reassure, amuse and reinforce, all of which she did with different students as they tackled each task.

This was a successful approach because the teacher was confident in her knowledge of the strong mutual respect that had already been established between her and these students. This had developed not just because of her personality but also as a consequence of her thorough preparation. She knew the students well and had extensive notes about individuals, such as prior qualifications (or lack of them) and other information that was relevant to their learning and behaviour. She used this well, for example by selecting certain students to demonstrate to others particular activities, such as changing the brushes on the cleaning equipment. She was aware that status was important and at no time posed questions or set tasks that would embarrass a student.

The students enjoyed the lesson, behaved maturely and enthusiastically demonstrated the required skills.

Commentary

The high expectations demanded by this teacher, in this particular setting, were fundamental to the success of this lesson. The students were more than willing to adapt to her requirements, not just because of the teacher's thorough planning and skilful practice but also as a consequence of the excellent relationships she had developed with them.

What did these students learn? In line with the planned outcomes, they gained specific competence-based cleaning skills. What was not in the lesson plan, though, was the fact that this took place within a framework of self-discipline, responsibility, aspiration and self-esteem. A key part of the lesson was the development of students' positive attitudes to doing a job of work and doing it well.

The fact that these students were unlikely to have been intrinsically motivated to learn how to clean when they started this course did not reduce the teacher's enthusiasm. Instead, she had won over the students by planning lessons in a way that kept them active. The tasks were sufficiently demanding to keep students interested, not so easy that they were insulted and not so difficult that students were intimidated. She also routinely linked activities and behaviour to future employment, subtly reminding students of the reasons why they needed to develop these skills. The checking of each student's level of competence was done discreetly so as not to allow assessment requirements to overshadow the lesson.

Reflecting the techniques described by Kounin (1977), the teacher demonstrated excellent classroom management skills, particularly 'a look' she used to remind students that a lack of interest or disruptive behaviour were not options worthy even of consideration.

Chapter summary

The quality of the work produced by the students in these four lessons reflects the high expectations of their teachers. The fact that the students worked to a high standard, remained motivated and did not misbehave was no accident. This was a direct consequence of the very skilful teaching techniques employed by the teachers and the strong relationships they had developed with their students. The 20 outstanding lessons in the book are a reminder that there does not need to be a clash between a focus on high standards and the lifelong learning sector's well-deserved reputation for being inclusive.

The sector has a long tradition of welcoming and accommodating students of all ages, abilities and backgrounds, and every institution can provide many examples of those who have succeeded, seemingly against all the odds.

Lesson summary (lessons 13–16)

Table 5.1   Lesson summary (lessons 13–16)

	Particular strengths
Lesson 13 Media studies	• Very high standard of students' work • Excellent use of well-designed brief, based on authentic commercial setting • Independent working by students in industrious atmosphere • Highly constructive feedback by teacher to each student, encouraging them to strive for high standards • Very knowledgeable and enthusiastic teacher
Lesson 14 Social work	• Excellent development of learners' reflective skills • High standard of learners' presentations • Very high standard of questioning and discussion by learners • Very good management of lesson by teacher, with skilful but minimal intervention as appropriate • Very good use of action plans to help learners to evaluate and inform their practice
Lesson 15 Hairdressing	• Very high standard of students' work, demonstrating application of theory to practice • Excellent communication skills of students • Outstanding management of lesson by teacher, with clear fit of clients to students' abilities and levels of expertise • Excellent questioning by teacher • Very good, and appropriately subtle, feedback given by teacher to students throughout the lesson
Lesson 16 Cleaning and support services	• Full involvement of students, all of whom demonstrated the required knowledge and skills • Excellent development of relationships • Outstanding classroom management by teacher, preventing disruption and encouraging a professional approach to each task • Enthusiastic and passionate teacher • Very thorough knowledge of students by teacher, used exceptionally well to plan lesson

6 Inclusive practice

Inclusive teaching and learning means different things to different people. In the school sector, it is primarily about the way in which pupils with special educational needs learn and are taught. In higher education institutions, it is frequently used to refer to the teaching of students with disabilities. However, Thomas and May (2010), in examining inclusive practice in higher education, describe an approach that focuses not on specific target groups or dimensions of diversity, but rather on striving towards proactively making education accessible, relevant and engaging to *all* students. Inclusive teaching and learning now tends to have a similarly broad meaning in the lifelong learning sector.

Diversity dimensions

The categorization of dimensions of diversity (Thomas and May 2010: 5), as outlined in Table 6.1, is useful in relation to the lifelong learning sector and to the debate as to what constitutes an inclusive lesson.

In reflecting on the combination of different factors that each contributed to making the 20 outstanding lessons inclusive, it is helpful to distinguish between two stages: before the lesson and during the lesson.

Inclusion – before the lesson

As with many other aspects of good practice, an inclusive approach starts with the planning of lessons. In deciding on how they would teach, the teachers had anticipated potential opportunities to involve all students, particularly those who they knew would be less likely or willing to engage. The reasons why students may have been reluctant to participate varied within and between the different lessons and incorporated aspects of all of the dimensions listed in Table 6.1. Active or experiential learning methods, as adopted in these lessons, lend themselves well to working cooperatively with fellow students and, when managed expertly, this encourages participation and minimizes exclusion.

Table 6.1 Diversity dimensions

Diversity dimensions	Examples
Educational	Level/type of entry qualifications; skills; ability; knowledge; educational experience; life and work experience; learning approaches
Dispositional	Identity; self-esteem; confidence; motivation; aspirations; expectations; preferences; attitudes; assumptions; beliefs; emotional intelligence; maturity; learning styles; perspectives; interests; self-awareness; gender; sexuality
Circumstantial	Age; disability; paid/voluntary employment; caring responsibilities; geographical location; access to IT and transport services; flexibility; time available; entitlements; financial background and means; marital status
Cultural	Language; values; cultural capital; religion and belief; country of origin/residence; ethnicity/race; social background

In the family learning lesson, described later in this chapter, the teacher had thought carefully in advance of the lesson about which learners should work together to minimize conflict and maximize learning opportunities. The animal care teacher had very clear ideas about the order in which students would do their presentations and, similarly, the social work teacher had planned to make sure that the most articulate student would be the first to present a review of her placement.

Sophisticated and planned questioning, as discussed in Chapter 4, helped to ensure the involvement of all students and avoid potential embarrassment or humiliation that could have alienated students.

A focus on enabling students to develop their literacy, numeracy and language skills is also important, as low attainment in these areas is a major barrier to future success. This was the primary purpose of the skills for life lesson, but teachers in the other lessons, too, planned to incorporate opportunities to develop and refine these skills, as was evident in the cleaning and support services, science and media studies lessons. In the human anatomy and physiology lesson, planning highlighted ways in which the learning support assistant could best provide English support for the two adults in the class who did not have English as their first language. The development of numeracy was successfully linked to the hospitality lesson and embedded in the construction lesson described later in this chapter.

In some lessons, opportunities were identified in advance to incorporate reference to the cultural dimensions of diversity. In the hospitality lesson, for example, the teacher raised the issue of kosher and halal methods of slaughter which generated, as planned, student interest in religions they were unfamiliar with and the art teacher directed students to artists from diverse ethnic backgrounds. As noted when discussing the planning of resources, attention had been paid to ensure that materials used did not reinforce any gender, ethnic or cultural stereotyping. The ESOL teacher, aware that he wanted to emphasize the diversity of the college to the monocultural, all-male group he had just started teaching, planned to use a video clip of male and female students of all nationalities.

Most importantly, in relation to what constitutes inclusive practice, teachers planned their lessons with high expectations for *all* of their students, as discussed in Chapter 5. This was made possible, in part, because teachers knew their students well, with the exception of the ESOL teacher, and they were aware of students' attainment levels. The skills for life teacher had prepared tailor-made material to meet the academic needs of her students. In the hairdressing salon, clients were allocated to students on the basis of each student's current skill level. The physics teacher knew precisely why each student had not been as successful as they could have been in the practice examination they had completed and the classical civilization teacher was keenly aware of his students' individual strengths and areas for development. Familiarity with students' recent and prior attainment, as well as background, was particularly important in the cleaning and support services lesson as it provided the teacher with the information she needed to explain certain behaviour and to ensure that she did not exclude anyone or cause them discomfort.

Supportive, empathetic and caring though these teachers were, they did not, as noted in relation to the skills for life lesson, prioritize 'soft' skills over 'hard' achievement in any of the lessons, thereby avoiding to some extent what Ecclestone and Hayes (2009) describe as a worrying psychotherapeutic trend in education towards a focus on seeing all students as vulnerable and in need of support. Many of the 20 lessons were highly successful in developing students' confidence and self-esteem, but this was in addition to, and not at the expense of, the acquisition of planned knowledge and academic and/or vocational skills.

The teachers of these 20 outstanding lessons had clearly thought about the most appropriate teaching and assessment methods for their students, on the basis of what they knew about them, what they wanted their students to learn and what they knew would work. While teachers matched tasks and questions to students' ability, and started from where the students were at, there was no evidence of them attempting to link this to an individual student's supposed learning style, using labels such as visual, auditory, kinaesthetic or active. The fact that they did not refer to, or base decisions on, models of learning styles prevalent in the sector over the last few decades would appear to support the very thorough research on this topic undertaken by Coffield et al. (2004a, 2004b) and their conclusion that these models are far too simplistic to be of any real value to either teachers or students.

Inclusion – during the lesson

An atmosphere of mutual respect was a strong feature of all the lessons. Reflecting the theory Y approach described in Chapter 5, teachers demonstrated through their language, actions, attitudes, gestures and humour that they valued all their students and this in turn had encouraged students to behave in a similarly respectful manner.

Teachers were adept at managing group and pair work as well as discussions in a way that encouraged participation and avoided exclusion, and they used opportunities as they arose to challenge stereotypes. This was particularly effective in the geography lesson, where the teacher skilfully wove into the debate educational, circumstantial, dispositional and cultural dimensions of diversity. In the motor vehicle studies lesson, the teacher challenged gender stereotypes by routinely making reference to female mechanics as well as males. The social work teacher had created an inclusive culture with her students and was confident in letting them address the issue of racism raised by one of the learners, without any intervention.

Four outstanding lessons

The final four lessons, as described below, demonstrate different aspects of inclusive practice. In the information technology lesson, the teacher introduced her learners to spreadsheets, paying particular attention to what these adults already knew and their motivation for attending the course. The construction teacher treated with great respect his group of school pupils who attended the college three days a week and had been labelled as disaffected. In the teacher education lesson, the teacher provided structured opportunities for her adult learners to reflect on aspects of assessment, drawing on their experience and practice. The final lesson, on family learning, with its focus on learning by both adults and children, epitomizes the kind of inclusion that has long been associated with the lifelong learning sector.

Lesson 17

Subject – information technology
Course/level – entry
Lesson length – two hours
Location – adult and community college
Number of students present – 15
Age – adults
Context – full-time course; 10 female and 5 male

All of the learners had completed a course relatively recently on word processing and/or using the internet. This was the first lesson on spreadsheets but the teacher already knew the learners from earlier courses.

The teacher started the lesson away from the computers with learners sitting around a table at the front of the room. She asked learners to introduce themselves and she checked the register while they were doing this. She then briefly spoke about herself and the nature of this five-session course. She explained that the task they had undertaken in the previous week when they had enrolled indicated that they all knew the basics of using a computer, for example opening, saving and printing files, editing text, copying and pasting, but she would assume that they were all beginners in relation to spreadsheets. This provoked very positive responses from the learners.

On an interactive whiteboard, the teacher showed a very simple budget in a spreadsheet and said they would be starting with this. She then showed two more, both of which looked more complex, suggesting that by the end of the lesson some of them would be tackling something similar. The teacher chose to ignore comments from the learners, who suggested they were unlikely to get to that stage and/or they were 'hopeless at maths'.

Learners moved from the front of the room to their computers and the teacher kept them all working together and at the same pace as they created the first spreadsheet. The teacher's own version of the simple budget appeared on the large screen as she entered the relevant text and numbers. As they got to the first total for weekly outgoings, the teacher asked them to work it out in their head or use a calculator. She did the same for income total and also disposable income total so that learners had to manually subtract total outgoings from income. This caused some amusement and eventually they agreed the figures and entered them onto their spreadsheet. The teacher then said that the rent had increased and so they needed to change that figure. The learners did this, but expressed frustration as they recognized the impact this would have on the total outgoings and also on the figure for disposable income.

At this point the teacher asked them to copy her as she typed into the relevant cells three formulae – one to total all the outgoings, another to total income and a third to subtract total outgoings from the income. On the screen, nothing changed and so one of the learners asked 'What's the point of that?' Instead of answering the question, the teacher asked the learners to implement yet another increase in rent. As they did so, and the other cells adjusted automatically to accommodate the rent increase, the learners were thrilled and several actually said 'aha' aloud as they realized how these formulae worked.

For the rest of the lesson, learners worked at their own pace, either on more extensive budgets, as provided by the teacher, or on their own finances. The tutor walked around supporting them and, on a few occasions, brought the group together to explain something or share a discovery made by one of the learners. It was evident that all learners had mastered the use of basic formulae and, more importantly, had ideas as to other potential uses of spreadsheets. One learner, having mastered the SUM formula, asked if there were a formula to calculate the average for a column or row. Instead of providing the answer, the teacher suggested he use the 'help function' to find out. He did this, experimented and was delighted with his own success. Others drew on their prior experience with other applications to experiment with aspects such as formatting cells.

Just before the end of the lesson, the teacher asked the learners to close their files and turn off their computers. This needed reinforcing several times, as learners wanted to continue. Once she had everyone's attention, the teacher showed the learners the same three spreadsheets on the large screen that she had presented at the beginning of the lesson. No comments were necessary. It had the desired effect of highlighting to the learners how much progress they had made in the lesson, particularly given their negative comments at the start.

Commentary

In this inclusive lesson, the teacher started from where the learners were at, in terms of their existing knowledge, skills and experience. She used an 'advance organizer' (Ausubel 1960), as discussed in relation to the human anatomy and physiology lesson described in Chapter 2, outlining what students would be doing in the lesson and how this new topic would build on what they already knew about information technology. Although these were motivated adult learners on the course of their own choosing, she was aware of their anxiety in tackling something new, particularly as it involved mathematics, which several of them felt uncomfortable with. She had planned the lesson extremely well to ensure that learners would realize by the end how much progress they had each made.

The teacher introduced spreadsheets, keeping all the learners together on the same activity, in a structured way, leading to the planned Gestalt insight moment, as discussed in Chapter 3, when the learners suddenly realized the main benefits of using formulae. After this, the teacher let the learners work at their own pace, applying what appeared to be a new found freedom to explore and discover additional features.

What did these students learn? They learned how to set up and use the basic features of a spreadsheet. However, the success of this lesson was not that these learners became familiar with as many spreadsheet features as possible, but rather that they learned how they could find things out for themselves. They learned how to learn. What mattered was not so much *what* they learned on this topic but *how* they did it. It also prompted suggestions as to how they might use spreadsheets in their personal and work lives.

The teacher's skill was in using a *guided* discovery learning approach to provide the stages and setting for the learners' 'aha' moment. This was not dissimilar to the way in which the numeracy teacher, in lesson 1, had guided her students to an understanding of an invoice. Pure discovery learning that involves leaving the learners to their own devices from the start without any guidance at all from the teacher may appear to be an attractive idea. However, it rarely works in practice within the constraints of a formal educational setting as it usually takes too much time. Often, students do not come to the 'right' conclusion although, depending on the purpose of the exercise, this may in itself be a desirable outcome.

Lesson 18

Subject – bricklaying
Course/level – entry
Lesson length – two and a half hours
Location – further education college
Number of students present – 15
Age – 14 to 16
Context – male pupils from local school attending the college three days a week

All the students arrived on time to the construction workshop and the teacher quickly checked relevant health and safety issues. Without prompting, the students put away their mobile telephones. They did not present any of the disruptive behaviour they had demonstrated in other educational institutions. Within five minutes, having checked the register and students' protective clothing, the teacher ensured that students were engaged in practical tasks.

The success of this lesson was due in no small measure to the teacher's consummate command of a potentially challenging group of students, most of whom were struggling at school and/or had rejected formal schooling. He had earned their complete respect through force of personality combined with vocational expertise and credibility, as well as through showing these students a high degree of respect.

The students thoroughly enjoyed the lesson. The teacher was able to devote all his time to helping them learn and develop practical skills without too many distractions. The students all expressed their hatred of mathematics at school, but when the teacher told them that they could not lay bricks properly without being able to perform basic calculations, they readily moved over to work at tables in the corner of the workshop for a brief period. Here they concentrated on a series of short, relevant calculations designed to improve their numeracy skills, following particularly clear explanations from the teacher.

The teacher set the highest standards for practical work, emphasizing the need for students to work both accurately and at speed. When students made mistakes, the teacher showed them how to correct them and made them practise again until the work reached industry standards. Once students got it right, the teacher's praise was fulsome and students took immense pride in their achievements. Those students who mastered the basics more quickly than others were immediately given more demanding practical tasks to perform.

Commentary

Another dual professional, this teacher demonstrated the kind of *with-it-ness* discussed in Chapter 5 in relation to classroom management. His manner and his brisk start to the lesson also reflect the importance of three of Smith and Laslett's rules (2001), as discussed in the previous chapter, for preventing potential disruption: 'get them in', 'get on with it' and 'get on with them'. The students knew that this teacher would not tolerate misbehaviour and they held him in high regard, seemingly relishing the self-discipline that he had instilled in them. With the practical tasks, the teacher made no allowances for students' low prior achievement, taking the view that all bricks must be laid perfectly, regardless of the background or age of the bricklayer.

What did these students learn? Students achieved the relevant practical competence, in line with the planned outcomes and syllabus requirements, as well as developing their numeracy knowledge and skills. Referring back to the second definition of learning in Chapter 1, the 'significant change' was in their attitude to the task, the teacher, each other and to their desire to succeed. Learning in the construction workshop, as opposed to a school classroom, was an important factor in that students were able to apply their newly acquired skills immediately. Given their negative associations with school, the importance of this type of situated learning context was likely to have been even more significant than it was for the students in the hospitality and hairdressing lessons.

The teacher was well aware of the fact that poor numeracy skills were a barrier to future success for these students and he was intent on helping them to improve their knowledge and skills, for their own benefit and to provide opportunities to obtain employment in this or any other area of work. He enabled them to do so by providing clear, contextualized explanations and practical and relevant numeracy tasks.

This aspect of the lesson reflects the discussion about how the *need* to learn can, at times, generate a genuine desire to learn. Some of the students, to their own surprise, enjoyed the numeracy tasks and most were visibly pleased when they made correct calculations and saw the impact of this on their brickwork. Linking the students' attitude to the expectancy theory discussed earlier, it seemed as if these students, having experienced so much failure in the past, genuinely expected to succeed on this particular course, and this in turn had the effect of increasing their motivation. This was in no small measure due to the teacher's belief in them.

Lesson 19

Subject – teacher education (preparing to teach)
Course/level – advanced
Lesson length – two hours
Location – further education college
Number of students present – 12
Age – adults
Context – part-time course; 10 female and 2 male teachers, from adult and
*   community learning, work-based learning, the charity and private sectors,*
*   as well as teaching in prisons*

Having welcomed the group and reminded them that this was the first of three lessons on assessment, the teacher distributed a handout to each trainee and asked them to read it quietly. It contained three different short essays, all entitled 'The role of the hotel manager'. The teacher explained that students on a tourism course had been asked to write essays on this topic and she would like trainees to mark these three essays, giving each a percentage grade. This request provoked an explosion of questions from the trainees, all speaking at once, but the teacher stopped them and said 'No questions yet – you've got 20 minutes and then we'll discuss it.'

After the 20 minutes, the teacher asked trainees to feed back their marks and it soon became apparent that there was little consensus. In fact, for one of the essays, the marks varied from 25 per cent to 80 per cent. The teacher then led a very lively and productive discussion, focusing on why it was so difficult to mark these essays and why there was such disparity among the markers. The trainees discussed the significance of subject knowledge, structure, accuracy, word length, fluency and spelling errors as well as the stage at which students were in their course when they completed this essay. The trainees all agreed that they needed some kind of criteria and/or marking scheme.

As people spoke, the teacher made notes on a pre-prepared grid on the interactive whiteboard under three columns. At the end of the discussion, she revealed the three headings, which were validity, reliability and fairness.

The trainees were then given criteria for the first essay and asked to read it again quietly and use the criteria to re-mark it. When they finished, the teacher initiated another whole-group discussion, which highlighted the fact that grades given by trainees this time, although not all the same, were much closer to each other than at the first attempt without the criteria. The discussion this time was set within the framework of validity, reliability and fairness, terms which the trainees now used with ease and accuracy.

Summarizing the lesson, the teacher reminded the group that the notes from today, as well as references for further reading on assessment, would be on the college's virtual learning environment and she alerted them to the homework task, which was to discuss an aspect of assessment in their own practice and subject specialism.

Commentary

This teacher, as a teacher educator, was keen to practise what she preached in terms of using the most appropriate teaching methods for this group of trainees and this topic.

Because these learners were adults and already employed part time as teachers, it would not be unreasonable to assume that they were all highly motivated. In effect, that was not the case as some of them had enrolled on the course because they needed the qualification. As with several of the previous lessons in this book, the teacher was gradually winning them over as they began to see the value of what they were learning, the fact that they enjoyed the lessons and, on this particular course, the realization that they could apply the techniques used by this teacher to their own teaching.

The teacher adopted an inductive approach, with a well-designed task as the catalyst to get learners to come to their own conclusions about assessment criteria and the associated issues for both teachers and students. This lesson provides another example of when it would have been inappropriate to inform learners at the start of the lesson of the learning outcomes. Had she told them they would be looking specifically at assessment criteria and marking schemes, it would have given the learners the 'answer' to the task she went on to give them.

What did these students learn? They gained a deeper understanding of the issues that affect and inform assessment from the teacher's and

students' points of view and also learned the meaning of associated terminology. They demonstrated their understanding by relating this to their
own experience as a student, as well as reflecting on how they might apply
what they had learned to their own practice as a teacher. As with the social
work, hairdressing and art and design learners, the development of their
reflective skills was recognized as an important factor in their role as professionals.

Lesson 20

Subject – family learning
Course/level – entry
Lesson length – 90 minutes
Location – community centre
Number of students present – 15
Age – adults
Context – part-time course; 13 female and 2 male

Parents, grandparents and carers were at ease entering the premises as
this was a location, next to the primary school, that they were familiar
with. Significant effort had been made to make it look inviting, with flow-
ers and plants in tubs as well as laminated murals of the work by adults
and children on the railings. The confident and friendly teacher offered
a warm welcome to the learners, who straggled in after leaving their children either at school or in the adjacent room with nursery or early years
workers.

Some found it hard to settle down initially. One mother was upset
due to a domestic issue but the teacher dealt with this kindly and speedily, directing her and the other learners to the biscuits, cakes and tea- and
coffee-making facilities in one corner of the room.

Those who had arrived early began to look at their folders and insert
the work they had brought with them, some of which was related to the
literacy and/or numeracy lessons they also attended at the same centre
on another day. While some chatted amicably to one another, the teacher
dealt skilfully with a child who wanted to stay with his mother. She
called for support from the nursery staff next door, who enticed the child
away.

Within six or seven minutes, all were settled and the teacher started
the lesson. The focus of this lesson was on how to read with your child. The
teacher, who knew these learners well, organized them into three groups of
four and one of three, carefully selected on the basis of the adults' language
and literacy level, age of their children and also the learners' interpersonal
and communication skills. Groups were given a set of instructions and a

choice of two children's books relevant to the age group they would be discussing. Each group allocated a leader to manage the task, which involved reading, digesting and discussing information about child development, reading levels and communication skills, which was given to them on a handout. After 20 minutes, individuals were given a card that explained their role. Each group had to undertake a role play exercise, with one person playing the child and another reading to her or him a short story. The remaining one or two people in the group were required to observe the role play and make notes on the extent to which the adult and child had behaved in terms of what the group had read and discussed earlier in the lesson. Aware of each person's literacy level and writing skills, the teacher discreetly gave some individuals a template for the notes but not others. Dictionaries and several computers were available in the room and these were used by a few learners during the activity.

The teacher circulated, joining each group in turn, answering questions, making the odd comment here and there but generally listening and observing rather than talking. The groups thoroughly enjoyed this activity, particularly those who played the role of the child and asked several 'awkward' questions.

After this, the teacher asked each group to identify one thing each individual had learned from the exercise and to write this on a large sheet of paper, which they then displayed on the wall. In the last five minutes, learners moved out of their groups, mingled and looked at what others had written. The issues identified included ones about learning new vocabulary, some about ways to modify the voice and tone and how to emphasize different words and others to do with asking and answering questions. Others wrote facts about child development.

The teacher informed them that their homework was to apply what they had learned in this lesson to the way they would read to their child in the next few days and then be prepared to talk at the next lesson about the impact this has on them and their child. Learners agreed that this seemed like a good idea.

Despite the seemingly relaxed and informal atmosphere, at no time did the teacher let the lesson lapse into casual chat. She, like the other teachers in the outstanding lessons, was *with-it* and fully aware of who was doing what in her lesson. She kept all the learners on task and took every opportunity to encourage them to challenge themselves and each other.

Commentary

This teacher was highly empathetic and very successfully created a supportive and inclusive learning environment. However, she balanced this extremely well with maintaining a focus throughout the lesson on her key aim, which was to develop learners' knowledge and skills so that they could read to and with their children with greater expertise and confidence. She demonstrated excellent classroom management skills. As well as skilful organization and monitoring of the group activities, she dealt very quickly and effectively with several potentially time-consuming situations as learners arrived, so as to start the lesson as soon as possible.

The teacher had prepared meticulously for this group of adults who had widely varying academic and social needs. The diversity of the group reflected differences in all four dimensions discussed earlier in this chapter: educational, dispositional, circumstantial and cultural. With its emphasis on personal development and mutual peer support, this lesson reflected the values and ideals most often associated with the tradition of adult learning.

The teaching and assessment approaches were similar to the one taken in the first lesson on numeracy. All groups worked on the same task at the same time but each had different reading books and slightly different instructions. Roles were allocated carefully, taking into account a variety of factors, including the fact that almost all the learners had little in the way of academic achievement and some, when they had started the course, had lacked the social confidence to participate in group activities.

What did these students learn? They extended their knowledge about child development and approaches to reading with children, as well as improving their own reading skills. They also learned in this lesson how to interact socially, digest and discuss the written information they were given and participate productively in group activities. There was very good evidence, through their work, attitudes and commitment to the course, to suggest that many were also acquiring a thirst for learning.

Chapter summary

Inclusive practice, as demonstrated in these four lessons, is not just about being nice to students and creating a pleasant learning environment, important though that is. It incorporates all the other themes in this book: thoughtful planning, carefully crafted questions, subject expertise, enthusiasm and high expectations for all students. The honest ways in which they contributed to discussions and reflected on their own progress suggests that students considered themselves to be in a safe and supportive environment. Whatever their age, gender, background or current circumstances, students in these lessons were taken seriously and they all made considerable progress in the development of their knowledge and skills.

Lesson summary (lessons 17–20)

Table 6.2   Lesson summary (lessons 17–20)

	Particular strengths
Lesson 17 Information technology	• Meticulously planned lesson • Inclusive, supportive climate • Considerable leap in learners' ability to apply what they learned in the lesson • Excellent development of learners' ability to learn and find out information for themselves • Excellent classroom management by teacher • Outstanding example of inductive and insight learning • Highly skilled, knowledgeable and enthusiastic teacher
Lesson 18 Bricklaying	• Excellent development of students' practical skills and work and study ethics • Highly inclusive climate of respect between teacher and students • Superb workshop management demonstrated by dual professional • Excellent questioning employed to elicit and develop students' knowledge and skills • Excellent development of students' numeracy skills, through well-devised and relevant tasks • Constructive feedback given to students throughout lesson
Lesson 19 Teacher education	• Excellent knowledge of topic demonstrated by trainee teachers • Inclusive climate • Very good application of inductive learning • Very well-structured and well-planned lesson • Excellent task used to good effect to promote discussion • Excellent management of discussion by teacher
Lesson 20 Family learning	• Very considerable development by learners in their knowledge and skills • Highly inclusive and supportive environment • Excellent task, devised to challenge and accommodate the range of learners present • Very good use of role play • Passionate, enthusiastic, empathetic and knowledgeable teacher

7 Characteristics of outstanding lessons

All 20 outstanding lessons have now been introduced and reviewed in the context of emerging themes but some key overarching questions remain. Does the evidence suggest that in order to be outstanding there is a typical type of lesson in terms of subject or setting or a typical type of student? Is there a typical type of teacher? Are there differences between teaching adults and teaching younger students? Are there typical teaching and assessment methods and is there one main philosophy or theory underpinning the lessons?

Subjects or settings

There is no typical type of outstanding lesson in this respect. By chance rather than design, as noted in the first chapter, the lessons are very different. They include 20 different subjects, of which four are A levels or AS levels, 12 are vocational, one is teacher education and the other three are adult and community learning courses. Thirteen of the lessons took place in general further education colleges, two in sixth-form colleges, three in community centres, one in a work-based learning provider and another in a young offenders' institution.

The one factor that *may* be of significance is class size. The average number of students in these lessons was approximately 17. The smallest group size was eight and the largest was 26. This is small, in comparison to both the school and higher education sectors. It does, however, reflect the lifelong learning sector at the time of the observations and many more lessons involving a similar number of students were *not* judged outstanding. It may well be the case, though, that it would be more difficult to be judged outstanding if teaching a significantly larger number of students. Gibbs (2012), focusing on higher education, argues that in an educational context, class size and the extent of close contact with teachers are two of the factors known to predict both student performance and learning gains.

The students in these 20 outstanding lessons certainly had the benefit of close contact with teachers who knew them well.

Students

There is no typical type of student. One of the lessons involved school pupils aged 14 to 16, 11 involved young students aged 16 to 18 and one included students aged between 16 and 24. Seven of the lessons were for adult learners. Students were studying on a full-time basis in 14 of the lessons and part time in six. Fourteen of the lessons included both male and female students and, of the other six, three were all-male and the other three were all-female.

The diversity of the students in these lessons incorporated difference across a number of dimensions, namely previous education, personal disposition, current circumstances and cultural heritage, as reflected in Table 6.1.

Learning resources

There is no typical type of learning resource. Resources ranged from minimal to extensive in terms of quantity, and from relatively mundane to innovative in relation to quality. They were limited in the social work, geography and classical civilization lessons but creative and imaginative in the science, skills for life and numeracy lessons. Resources were of a commercial standard in the computer suite, college kitchen, hairdressing salon and construction workshop. They were very real in the animal care lesson.

In terms of technology, the media studies and introduction to spreadsheets lessons were based around the use of computers. Most teachers used interactive whiteboards and many made reference to their institution's virtual learning environment. Several of the other lessons involved the occasional use of computers but there were no examples of the transformational nature of technology in education, about which much has been written over the last few decades. This may be due to the selection of lessons or the period during which the observations took place. It may simply reflect research into the use of digital technologies in the school classroom (Luckin et al. 2012), which suggests that the key to their success, as with any other kind of traditional resource, is the *way* in which they are used. Technology, Luckin et al. argue, has to accompany innovative and structured teaching in order to have a true impact on educational achievement.

Age

Is there a difference between the teaching of young students and adults? Although some of the lessons involving younger students required tighter classroom management, such as in the statistics, cleaning and support services and bricklaying lessons, there was little difference in terms of teaching styles and assessment methods. The teachers of adult learners certainly applied the principles of the andragogical model as discussed in Chapter 5 and elsewhere throughout the book.

Andragogy emphasizes the fact that adults become more self-directed as they mature, but the younger students in these lessons demonstrated that they could be as self-directed as adults. This was particularly evident in the hospitality, art and design, motor vehicle studies, animal care, media studies and hairdressing lessons, where the students' mature approach appeared largely to be a product of the teaching, rather than a prerequisite.

One of the distinctions Knowles (1980) makes between pedagogy and andragogy is that the former fails to take sufficient account of students' experience. Interestingly, though, this was not the case in the outstanding lessons. For example, the geography teacher drew on students' experiences of daily life in their neighbourhood, limited though it was when compared to adult learners, to review urban planning options. The classical civilization teacher, too, at one point in the lesson started from where the students were at by looking at popular soap opera storylines. In the media studies lesson, the teacher asked students to reflect on their experiences of using the websites of organizations they were interested in, so that they could draw on that experience to inform their own designs.

Teachers

From the descriptions provided by HMI it is clear that there is no typical teacher in terms of age, gender, length of teaching experience or seniority. As noted in earlier chapters, they all demonstrated enthusiasm or passion in their own way. The nearest any of them came to being caricatures of charismatic and inspirational teachers were the geography and bricklaying teachers. Many of the teachers had a commanding classroom presence and, in terms of personality, a few would be considered as extravert, for example the teachers of both the statistics and cleaning and support services lessons. Several of the teachers used humour to good effect to increase students' attention or interest, diffuse potentially difficult discussions or situations and to create a positive environment. Humour, though, appears not to be an essential ingredient of an outstanding lesson, as some of the teachers were much more serious but equally effective. The media studies teacher, for example, was particularly unassuming.

In reflecting on the approaches these teachers took, it is helpful to use the three levels of thinking about teaching espoused by Biggs (1999: 21–4). At each level the focus changes, from *what the student is* at level 1, to *what the teacher does* at level 2 and, finally, to *what the student does* at level 3. Teachers who operate at level 1 acknowledge differences between students and see their responsibility as making the content of what they teach as clear as possible. It is then up to the students to attend lessons and to undertake the work given to them. The teachers' assumptions are that some students will do better than others, due to factors outside the control of the teacher, such as lack of motivation, low prior attainment, challenging social circumstances and innate ability.

Teachers at level 2, however, recognize the importance of employing a wider range of teaching methods to do more than just transmit information. They acknowledge the need to motivate students and maintain their interest and so they adjust their approach to one that they feel will be more effective. However, their focus remains on teaching strategies. At level 3, this focus shifts to what the student does. Teachers are clear, at this level, about what they want their students to do, say or produce, and to what standard, to demonstrate their understanding of what they have learned. Biggs suggests that teachers engage with these approaches at different points in their teaching career and that some may progress to level 3, while others remain at levels 1 or 2. One might reasonably argue that few teachers in the lifelong learning sector adopt the level 1 approach to their practice but many exemplify the type of teaching associated with level 2.

A common feature of the outstanding lessons in this book is that the teachers were operating much more in line with the level 3 approach than with the other two levels.

Teaching methods

There were typical types of method in that all the teachers employed some kind of active or experiential learning, regardless of the age of their students, the subject or the setting. There were certainly commonalities in what the teachers did *not* do. In the 20 outstanding lessons, there were no lectures or long periods of exposition by the teacher. Extensive note-taking did not feature; neither did dictation by the teacher nor copying text from a whiteboard. Students were not left to watch a video or sit by the computer for no apparent reason and they were never unsure as to what to do or why. They were not required to undertake any *purposeless* tasks, activities, discussions, group or pair work and at no point in time were they or the teacher left with nothing to do. There were no lulls in momentum, no disruptive behaviour and no sense of having to rush to 'get through' the syllabus.

Of particular note is the fact that the teachers of outstanding lessons spent as much time listening and observing as they did talking. Students were productively busy in the lessons. There were, in total, around 330 students in the lessons observed and not a single one of these students avoided meaningful participation.

The most frequently used teaching methods were:

- teaching based on problem-solving tasks
- teaching through questions and discovery, rather than telling
- teaching based on involvement in real, authentic tasks
- structured discussions, group and pair work
- letting students get on with it on their own.

Teaching based on problem-solving tasks

Teachers chose this approach in 12 of the 20 lessons, often in combination with the other methods discussed below.

In the two science lessons – human anatomy and physiology, and physics – students' understanding was developed through participation in a series of practical problem-solving tasks, from which they were able to extrapolate information and make generalizations. This encouraged students' curiosity and built on what they already knew. The teacher of the numeracy lesson for students with learning difficulties and/or disabilities created an innovative task, through which students at differing levels were able to make notable progress and enjoy themselves in doing so. In the media studies lessons, students grappled with the problems associated with designing a website within the framework of the real client brief they had been given, while the art and design students interpreted their brief in a variety of creative ways.

Each individual learner in the skills for life lesson had their own problems to solve, including everyday tasks around measurement, cooking and travelling as well as ones linked to job applications. The task of reflecting on the urban planning proposal in the geography lesson prompted a whole series of stimulating discussions, while the ESOL students tackled problem-solving tasks that would have an immediate impact on their ability to navigate around the college and their timetable.

Teaching through questions and discovery, rather than telling

Teachers used this approach in most of the lessons. In the classical civilization lesson, for example, the teacher elicited themes in the play being studied through questions, rather than by expounding information. The statistics teacher chose not to start the lesson by explaining the meaning of standard deviation but used questions to get students to the point where they began to understand the concept and only then asked them to apply the calculation. Instead of explaining how formulae work in a spreadsheet, the information technology teacher let students discover this for themselves. Rather than talk about assessment, the teacher educator asked questions about the way in which the learners had marked the essay she had given them, in order to elicit the knowledge she had wanted to impart about assessment criteria.

This is not to suggest that the teachers imparted no knowledge. It was cleverly interspersed into discussions and responses and also in the whiteboard notes in many lessons. There was no sense in any of the lessons of teachers rushing to get through lots of content. In some cases, the teachers did engage in short periods of exposition and demonstrate practical skills, for example in the hospitality, bricklaying and cleaning and support services lessons. This they did very effectively.

Teaching based on involvement in real, authentic tasks

Five vocational lessons – in motor vehicle studies, cleaning and support services, bricklaying, hospitality and hairdressing – were based on authentic tasks and the last two involved working with real clients. In these lessons, as discussed in earlier chapters, teachers were using a variety of teaching methods including demonstration, observation and questioning.

The use of role play cuts across the former category and this one, as in each of the three lessons in which this practice was used it was based on an authentic activity. In the numeracy lesson, it involved only one student but the benefit accrued to the whole group, who felt very much part of the exercise. In the ESOL lesson, it prepared students well for a time when they would need to use a telephone to contact the college to inform someone of their absence. In the family learning lesson, as well as being fun, the exercise was preparation for the very real activity of learners reading with their children.

Structured discussions, group and pair work

Whole-group discussions, pair and small group work and presentations were all structured. The whole-group discussions in the teacher education, geography and classical civilization lessons were teacher led and they were managed with considerable skill to ensure the involvement of all students and to maintain momentum and intellectual rigour. Activities undertaken in pairs in the numeracy, physics, ESOL, geography and motor vehicle studies lessons had a very clear purpose, as did group work in the family learning lesson.

Letting students get on with it on their own

In some of the lessons, teachers had enabled students to develop the skills to work independently and at their own pace. This was evident in the skills for life, art and design and media studies lessons, where the students were highly motivated and adept at working in this way. Similarly, where most of the lesson was given over to presentations by students, as in the animal care and social work lessons, the teacher had prepared the students particularly well in previous weeks and they, in turn, worked hard and very effectively. There appears to be no difference between adult learners and younger students in this respect, as these examples highlight.

Assessment methods

Was there a typical assessment method? Questioning featured, to varying degrees, in all the lessons and this is why a chapter is devoted to that particular assessment method. The high level of skills demonstrated by teachers with regard to questioning has been discussed in Chapter 4. A variety of other methods were also used, as reflected in the assessment grid in Table 7.1. These involved students completing written tasks and a variety of problem-solving activities to develop and assess knowledge and skills. Others focused on students' presentations and role play as mechanisms to assess understanding. Observation was used to ascertain students' vocational competence and peer assessment was employed very effectively.

In terms of assessment, the 20 lessons had the following features in common:

- A strong alignment of teaching, learning and assessment methods.
- The use of assessment to demonstrate both **declarative** and **practical** knowledge.
- Valid assessment tasks.
- A focus by the teacher on the development of subject knowledge and skills, rather than on the need to pass a summative assessment.
- High-quality feedback as a consequence of ongoing formative assessment.
- Assessment to encourage deep learning.

Table 7.1 Assessment methods used in the 20 lessons

Lesson	Question and answer	Written task(s)	Competence-based task	Contribution to debate	Problem-solving task	Students' presen-tation	Creative artefact	Role play	Formal peer assessment	Informal peer assessment
1	✓	✓		✓	✓			✓		✓
2	✓	✓			✓					✓
3	✓	✓			✓					
4	✓			✓	✓					
5	✓		✓	✓	✓					
6	✓						✓			
7	✓	✓								
8	✓	✓								
9	✓	✓		✓	✓					✓
10	✓			✓	✓					
11	✓		✓	✓	✓				✓	
12	✓	✓		✓	✓	✓		✓	✓	✓
13	✓				✓	✓				✓
14	✓			✓	✓	✓				✓
15	✓		✓	✓	✓					
16	✓		✓	✓	✓					
17	✓		✓		✓					✓
18	✓	✓			✓					
19	✓	✓		✓	✓			✓		✓
20	✓	✓			✓					✓

Alignment

In all of the 20 lessons, there was a close alignment of learning outcomes, assessment tasks and teaching methods that provided opportunities to get students to the point at which they could undertake the assessment tasks with confidence that they would succeed. Although referring primarily to course design rather than individual lessons, this is what Biggs (1999) refers to as '**constructive alignment**'. Because it happened so seamlessly in the outstanding lessons and there was no other control group with which to compare these lessons, it would be easy to minimize the role of the teacher in so skilfully creating and implementing this tight alignment.

In the absence of a control group, one might imagine less effective teachers tackling these 20 lessons in a very different way. For example, another art and design teacher may have been less forthcoming and skilful with feedback and, as a consequence, the students' final pieces and sketchbooks would not have been of such a high quality. Other science teachers might have worked through written examples and perhaps shown video clips, but would not have involved students in such a wide range of practical activities to ensure a certain depth of understanding. Different numeracy, bricklaying, hospitality and statistics teachers may have typically asked their students to plough through a series of numeracy worksheets and handouts. Students would have been keen to get the answers right but this would not necessarily have enabled them to understand the relevant mathematical concepts. The teachers may not have contextualized so carefully the mathematical problems they used, thereby making it more difficult for students to relate concepts to their existing knowledge and to the next stage of their work.

Other teachers of the theory lessons may have focused more on exposition, note-taking and written responses. They may also have used assessment methods to check students' recall of facts rather than the application of their understanding. Students might have associated 'learning' with guessing what the teacher wanted or expected or with ticking off generic, relatively meaningless targets they had been set. Others teaching vocational skills, as in the motor vehicle studies, hospitality, hairdressing, cleaning and support services and bricklaying lessons, may have helped to develop students' competence in relation to specific tasks but not asked as many carefully planned and sequenced questions to check how well students would be able to apply those skills in a different context. The information technology and media studies students, with different teachers, may have found themselves sitting at computers and following instructions in handouts and booklets, without giving too much thought to what they were doing or why. In such circumstances, they would certainly not have been as motivated or productive as they were in the lessons described in this book.

Different family learning and skills for life teachers may well have been empathetic and established a good rapport with their learners, but they might not have demanded such high standards, particularly in relation to the strong alignment of outcomes, assessment and teaching methods.

In effect, in many of the 20 outstanding lessons, teaching, learning and assessment were so intertwined that it is difficult to disentangle them. This was evident, for example, in the way in which teachers taught, incorporated and assessed numeracy and language development.

Numeracy

Teachers enabled students to develop their numeracy knowledge and skills explicitly in seven of the lessons. Clearly, mathematics was the focus of the numeracy and statistics lessons but it was also a feature of the hospitality, bricklaying, physics and information technology lessons. In the skills for life lesson, too, many of the learners had enrolled on the course in order to improve their numeracy.

The physics students were required not just to perform calculations but to explain to the teacher and to each other what they did and why, and how this informed their understanding of wave phenomena. Although the purpose of this was to prepare them for the written part of their forthcoming examination, it also provided an opportunity to check the accuracy and depth of students' mathematical understanding. In the statistics lesson, the teacher made sure, through expert questioning, that the students were clear about the concept of standard deviation before she gave them the formula, which they then used correctly to apply to business-related examples. In the numeracy lesson, students were so absorbed in the assessment task that they hardly realized they were learning about addition, subtraction and multiplication and accurately applying their knowledge and skills to a real-life problem. Those learners who were studying numeracy in the skills for life lessons demonstrated the depth of their learning in a variety of ways. One such learner, for example, was pleased when she realized she could apply what she had learned to temperature and currency conversions in relation to Slovakia, as this was where she was born and she had relatives there. The fact that the assessment tasks had been adapted by the teacher to be relevant to her provided added impetus and interest in the outcome of the calculations.

Both young students in the bricklaying workshop and some of the adults in the information technology lesson confessed to a strong dislike of mathematics. In both cases, though, the teachers won them round to realizing that it was not as difficult as they first thought. The bricklaying students knew they needed to make calculations for their potential employment, not just for the sake of it, and they had full trust in their teacher to help them in this respect. The adults, having learned how to create a spreadsheet, saw the potential of this tool for use in their everyday lives, with suggestions about running their own business, personal budgeting, travel claims and a variety of other forms of record keeping. The hospitality students, having cooked 300 ballotines earlier in the day, were keen to calculate how much the ingredients cost, the price customers had paid and therefore what, if any, profit was made by the college. Contextualization is not always the most appropriate approach, but in all of these lessons it was central to the motivation of the students to learn and to deepen their understanding of mathematics.

Language development

As well as the focus on literacy in the skills for life lesson and English in the ESOL lesson, teachers also incorporated contextualized language development into almost all the other lessons. Teachers in several lessons, as well as the learning support assistants in two of the lessons, paid attention to spelling and grammar, either by highlighting potential difficulties or by correcting errors, with explanations. Improving written expression and fluency was an important factor in the physics lesson, with students working in pairs to support each other on this.

There were plenty of examples of students developing their language skills by acquiring terminology that had been unfamiliar at the start of the lesson. Numeracy students, for example, applied vocabulary that was new to them to describe mathematical operations, as did the statistics students. Hospitality, motor vehicle studies, hairdressing and bricklaying students used newly acquired technical terms appropriately. Learners in both the teacher education and family learning lessons framed their discussions around terms they had not known prior to these lessons. Media studies students were encouraged to use, but not rely on, technology to improve the quality of their material in terms of spelling, grammar and style.

Oral skills were developed too, through participation in discussions, such as in the geography, classical civilization and teacher education lessons, as well as presentations in both the animal care and social work lessons.

Assessment of practical knowledge

In making decisions about the most appropriate assessment method to use, teachers of the outstanding lessons were clear not just about what they wanted their students to learn but also how they would go about checking that students could apply their newly acquired knowledge and skill. Students acquired both *declarative* knowledge, the sort that can be declared in written tasks or orally, for example in response to a question, as well as demonstrating *practical* knowledge in a variety of ways. Biggs (1999) refers to this as **functioning** knowledge, as it enables students to put to use what they have learned. Unsurprisingly, this was most evident in the practical, vocational lessons, where the choice of assessment method was more obvious, but it was also apparent in the theory lessons. For example, the role play exercise to read a children's story in the family learning lesson provided an opportunity for the learners to apply what they had read and discussed. One could also argue that the art and design students demonstrated functioning knowledge when they applied their research and ideas to creative artefacts, as did the students in the classical civilization lesson when they linked the work of Aristophanes to current political events.

Competence-based assessment has given rise to much debate over the last few decades as to its merits and worth not just in the lifelong learning sector but also in schools and higher education. Four common concerns about this method of assessment are highlighted by Armitage et al. (2007: 152). The first relates to *levels* of competence. Many people are familiar with the argument that if you need a plumber or a doctor, you want one who is at least good (ideally excellent), and not someone who is simply 'competent'. The second issue relates to a perceived focus on performance and behaviour rather than on the cognitive aspects underpinning that behaviour. The third concern is around reliability of the assessors' judgements and the fourth relates to the way in which this type of assessment drives learning and leads to a 'tick box' mentality. Experienced observers of lessons in the lifelong learning sector will be only too familiar with these problems.

Judged to be outstanding, the six lessons in this book that incorporated competence-based assessment did not include any of these common pitfalls. As emphasized in Chapter 5, the teachers all had high expectations of their students and demanded a standard of work that was certainly higher than just 'competent'. This was evident in the hospitality, motor vehicle studies, hairdressing, cleaning and support services, bricklaying and information technology lessons. In each case, the teacher paid considerable attention to ensuring that students did more than passively perform certain skills. They encouraged students to question, explore and evaluate in order to gain the underpinning knowledge they needed to shape, inform and justify their practice. The same standards were applied to all students, and although there was some evidence of ticking off competences, neither students nor teachers were rushing through tasks in order to tick them off.

Assessment validity

In all the lessons, the assessment tasks were valid. Validity, in terms of assessment, is taken to mean the extent to which a test measures what it is supposed to measure (Cox and Harper 2001). A written essay, for example, would not have been a valid tool to measure how well students in the information technology lesson could create a spreadsheet or the skill with which the students in the cleaning and support services lesson could change the brushes on the machine they were using. In the animal care lesson, the teacher might have chosen to ask each student to write a short essay on the care of their particular animal and then marked and returned it with comments. This has an element of validity and would not have been an unusual approach, but it would have assessed only declarative knowledge. Even then, it would not be entirely clear how much of the work was the students' own and how much was taken or even copied from a book, handout or internet site. By arranging for the students to present their research, she gave them the opportunity to ask each other questions, thereby assessing the quality and quantity of students' research and testing their declarative and functioning knowledge. That the students enjoyed the challenge and learned from each other was an added bonus.

Focus on knowledge and skills

Despite the fact that assessment usually drives the curriculum and that this in turn too often determines what happens in a lesson, a common feature in 19 of the 20 lessons was that teachers focused on the development of knowledge and skills in their subject and not on tests or examinations. Teachers did not start their lessons by declaring that they would cover a particular topic in order to pass a test or simply because it was in the syllabus. This is not to suggest that teachers were not adequately preparing their students for summative assessments. They were, but they did not make the students think that this was the *primary* purpose of the lesson. Examination preparation was most explicit in the physics lesson. It was implicit in many of the lessons and disguised well in some, such as in the classical civilization lesson.

There was no evidence in the lessons observed of students being driven, or motivated, by quantitative or qualitative targets. Teachers' practice in relation to the creation, promotion and use of target-setting for individual students was mixed. In over half the lessons, no reference was made at all to target-setting, although this does not mean that this process did not exist or form part of tutorial discussions. Minimum target grades for students on the AS level or A level courses in geography, classical civilization, physics and media studies were available in the documentation accompanying the lesson plans but not used overtly in the lessons observed.

Targets were used helpfully to contribute to assessment for learning in the following lessons: numeracy, skills for life, social work and hairdressing. The approach taken by teachers and students to formulating and using the targets in these lessons varied. The students in the numeracy lesson each had specific targets, identifying mathematical operations they were expected to be able to complete by the end of the lesson. Prior to the lesson, the teacher had very adeptly aligned these to the individual students and the tasks she had prepared for them, to ensure that the targets would be meaningful and achievable. They were checked discreetly at the end of the lesson. In the skills for life lesson, learners also had targets but the teacher had taken a different approach. Towards the end of the lesson, as in previous weeks with this group, she negotiated targets with each learner, skilfully helping them to diagnose where they were in terms of attainment levels and providing suggestions, but balancing this with giving learners the final say. Reflecting on their work placement and how it related to their course and their practice, the social work learners were fully in control of the targets they set themselves, with no intervention in this respect from their tutor. The hairdressing students had syllabus-related targets and took time at the end of their lesson to reflect on their progress and what they needed to do next. Although quite instrumental and focused on a list of competences, the students had developed their reflective skills well and were able to make considered judgements about the *quality*, not just quantity, of their work. Their targets, therefore, were meaningful to them as well as to their teacher.

An 'administrative' – and perhaps somewhat cynical rather than educational – approach to target-setting was evident in both the motor vehicle studies and bricklaying lessons. These students had targets which were taken directly from relevant course documentation and these were ticked off speedily by the teachers during the lessons. They did not have any impact on what the students did or did not do, but in neither case did this detract from what were otherwise excellent lessons. This approach, though, does highlight the problems often associated with target-setting. Martinez (2001) cites a range of research projects to support his argument for the implementation of target-setting across the sector. In the hands of expert practitioners, as in the four lessons discussed above, target-setting can indeed be used very effectively as a mechanism to advance students' learning as well as determine what they have already learned. However, experienced observers will have come across many examples of targets that are so generic they cannot be measured or so easy that they are not worth measuring. At worst, the procedure itself is used as a substitute for teaching and learning. This type of practice breeds a high degree of cynicism for both teachers and students and inevitably leads to a surface approach to learning whereby the purpose of the lesson or tutorial is simply to tick off targets.

Formative feedback

There were elements of summative assessments in the 20 outstanding lessons, for example the tasks in the motor vehicle studies, hospitality and hairdressing lessons. In these lessons and in the media studies lesson, where the students were completing a task that would contribute to a final assignment, the distinction between formative and summative assessment became somewhat blurred. A very strong feature of all the lessons, though, was the high quality of formative feedback and 'feed forward' given to students, mostly by the teacher but in several cases by other students too. Expert feedback to each individual in the art and design lesson, for example, was central to its success and to the high standard of students' work. This was the case, too, for the skills for life learners. The teachers' regular, constructively critical feedback throughout the bricklaying and cleaning and support services lessons was essential in maintaining the students' positive attitude and sense of pride in their work.

Deep learning

Tight alignment, assessment of practical knowledge, validity and formative assessment all contributed to encouraging the students to develop a **deep approach to learning** and assessment. Deep and surface learning were touched on in Chapter 2 and, as all 20 lessons have now been described, it is evident that neither the teachers nor the students displayed the signs of a surface approach. As noted in an earlier chapter, students who adopt a surface approach cut corners to get tasks over and done with quickly and out of the way and they are more likely to express negativity or cynicism about the activities they are asked to undertake. Teachers encourage this surface approach if they present tasks that are too easy or too difficult, allocate insufficient time to complete activities, rush through material to ensure appropriate coverage or suggest that students might not like the topic or the assessment but that they have to do it anyway.

Instead, the students in these 20 lessons enjoyed and, in some cases, even relished the opportunities they were given through assessment to make sense of what they were learning. While some might argue that there is an inherent tension between deep learning and outcomes-based education, the teachers of these 20 lessons did successfully encourage students to take a deep approach to their learning, through well-designed tasks and astutely aligned teaching methods. Ramsden (2003: 53) suggests that *what* students learn is closely associated with *how* they go about learning it. He goes on to argue that deep approaches are related to high-quality outcomes and they are also more enjoyable, while surface approaches are dissatisfying and linked to poor outcomes.

Theories or approaches

The literature on learning theories provides no consensus as to how to group certain theories or individuals or the extent to which they overlap or fit into distinct categories. There is, though, general agreement on two broad orientations, with behaviourism on one side and constructivism on the other. In between, or alongside, lies a whole host of other theories, such as neo-behaviourism, Gestalt theory, cognitivism and **humanistic psychology**, as well as situated learning, social learning theory and social constructivism. In the context of the two extreme orientations, there seems to be an assumption by educationalists that constructivism, most frequently linked to discussion, group work and process, is 'good'. Behaviourism, by the same token is perceived to be 'bad', associated as it is with outcomes, the transmission of information and a mechanistic form of training students to behave in a certain way, without them thinking or challenging what they are doing.

Nearer to behaviourism

Criticized by many as being controlling, 'teacher centred' and outdated, behaviourist elements were evident, to varying degrees, in all 20 outstanding lessons. Behaviourism has its origins in the early 20th century. This theory about learning, as espoused by Pavlov (1927), Watson (1928), Tyler (1949) and Skinner (1974), focuses on observable behaviour and is most widely associated with principles relating to stimulus–response, reinforcement and repetition.

First and foremost, the teachers had all identified in their lesson plans behaviourist learning outcomes. In this, of course, they had no choice in that it is the norm in the sector, as discussed in the first and second chapters. As is usual practice, the learning outcomes were broadly based on Bloom's taxonomy, as discussed in Chapters 2 and 4. The teachers of outstanding lessons used the full range of the taxonomy, although inevitably the extent of the range varied from lesson to lesson, depending on the subject and the level of the course. Examples of these outcomes are provided in Table 2.1 in Chapter 2.

The problems associated with learning outcomes were raised in Chapter 2. In using them, there is an assumption that it is possible to represent knowledge in the form of a list of behaviours. There is a view that this approach encourages the use of trivial and narrow outcomes, as these are easier to measure. Having to define them, narrow or not, before the lesson limits opportunities to deviate and explore issues raised by students. However, there are also advantages to having clear statements of what students are expected to achieve and how they will demonstrate that achievement. Acceptance of this approach may, as noted earlier, be due to its simplicity but it may also be linked to the fact that learning outcomes have now become fully embedded as 'common currency' in the world of education.

Behaviourists assert that positive or negative feedback will lead to a strong association with the stimulus and the desired behaviour. In teaching and learning, this means that students will repeat behaviour if they receive positive feedback because that behaviour is what teachers want them to display. Conversely, they will not repeat the behaviour if they get negative feedback.

The teachers of the outstanding lessons provided feedback quickly to students and used a range of 'reinforcers'. For example, and as noted in Chapter 4, most of the teachers rewarded students with praise when they made positive contributions to discussions, provided a correct answer or completed a task well. The ESOL teacher developed his own reinforcers. The positive one was a thumbs up while the negative one was an index finger to his mouth to indicate that he wanted the learners to stop talking. Overall, there was far less evidence of negative reinforcers, although a few teachers used non-verbal gestures to prevent potential disruption, as described in Chapter 5. The idea of intermittent reinforcement, a principle of behaviourism, was also evident in that several teachers gave praise more frequently early on in lessons, particularly those involving the development of practical skills, but did not reward every positive response thereafter.

Unsurprisingly, the behaviourist approach is most evident in the vocational lessons on skills development, with its instrumental and pragmatic focus. In conditioning their students to behave like chefs, mechanics, bricklayers, hairdressers and cleaners, teachers were concentrating on observable behaviour. Repetition, too, is a key feature of behaviourism. One of the most obvious examples of a seemingly traditional behaviourist approach was the hospitality lesson in which the teacher described what he wanted the students to produce. He demonstrated each step of the process and, as students copied his demonstration, he provided them with feedback at each stage. Students then went on to repeat the whole process 19 more times. This lesson was not that dissimilar in structure to the bricklaying lesson.

One could argue that, in other types of lesson, students had also been conditioned, albeit more subtly, to behave in a certain way. For example, students had learned to work independently in some lessons, they were used to periods of silence after questions in others and they kept to agreed

contracts or ground rules, such as in the animal care and cleaning and support services lessons.

In all these respects, it is possible to see the advantages of the approaches taken. Lesson planning around outcomes had enabled the teachers to plan their lessons in a structured way. Students were clear as to what was expected of them. The step-by-step approach with demonstration, practice and repetition worked well in the skills development lessons. Positive reinforcement was well received by the students in all lessons and led to the behaviour teachers desired. It was particularly effective in terms of behaviour management to avoid potential disruption in the bricklaying and cleaning and support services lessons. However, the teachers of outstanding lessons did much more than simply apply behaviourist principles.

Towards constructivism

Many of the assumptions associated with the humanistic approach to teaching and learning are embedded in the everyday practice and language of those who work in the lifelong learning sector. Influenced by Knowles (1980) and Rogers (1983), the emphasis on intrinsic motivation and the uniqueness of individuals and their self-concept was instrumental in the move towards 'student-centred' teaching and learning. The principles of andragogy, as discussed in Chapter 5, are prevalent in the sector and considered to be good practice. For example, it is common practice for teachers to be empathetic, to create very welcoming and positive learning environments, to promote collaboration and self-assessment and to describe themselves not as teachers but as 'facilitators of learning'.

None of the teachers of the outstanding lessons approached their teaching in a way that would suggest that they thought their students were there simply to receive information or to learn how to perform certain tasks.

In contrast to behaviourists, who place their emphasis on observable behaviour, cognitivists focus on how students gain and organize knowledge. The teachers of outstanding lessons acknowledged this in different ways. For example, they used 'advance organizers' (Ausubel 1960), as in the human anatomy and physiology lesson. In this lesson, as in others, the teacher provided students with an outline of what they intended to cover before going into detail, so that students could see the bigger picture and fit the new knowledge they would gain into a pattern. References have also been made to how teachers provided students with opportunities to gain insights or make patterns through guided discovery learning. In the information technology lesson, for example, the teacher started the lesson in what seemed to be a very behaviourist manner, taking a step-by-step approach to setting up a spreadsheet. Acknowledging the experience and knowledge her learners already had in relation to other aspects of information technology, she then went on to teach them *how* to solve problems themselves and how to become independent learners. In the second half of the lesson, she became far less directive and encouraged the learners to freely explore, based on their own interests and level.

Developing a model of how the world works by relating new knowledge to existing knowledge is a key assumption of constructivism, which has its origins in cognitive psychology. This suggests that, despite sitting in the same lesson and being exposed to the same teaching, each individual student constructs her or his own meaning. This may explain why after a lecture, however well structured and stimulating, the individuals in the audience, influenced by their experience, values, beliefs and existing knowledge, will leave with different interpretations of what they have learned. Similarly, 12 people on a jury will hear the same evidence from the defence and prosecution but will not necessarily come to the same conclusion as to the innocence or guilt of the accused.

Constructivists would argue that in addition to, or rather than, adding more knowledge, teachers may in fact be modifying the existing knowledge of their students. A constructivist perspective acknowledging that what students currently believe is important was evident in the geography lesson, where the teacher worked with students to reflect on their views and those of their peers, rather than simply imposing his own stance on the topic. In doing so, there was evidence to suggest the transformation of existing knowledge for many of the students. In the teacher education lesson, the trainees adjusted what they knew about their own disciplines and expertise to accommodate what they learned about assessment. Similarly, the approach taken in the social work lesson was based on a constructivist model, requiring each learner to identify what their placement meant to them and how they had changed as a consequence of that experience.

While a seemingly behaviourist approach was adopted in relation to classroom management in several lessons, as noted earlier, it was tempered by teachers trying to understand the students' point of view, creating friendly and productive relationships and also helping students to develop a positive view of themselves. This was particularly evident in both the cleaning and support services and bricklaying lessons. Praise was used to reward behaviour but it was applied judiciously and sincerely. Similarly, in the other skills development lessons, teachers did not just focus on observable behaviour, important though that was. They did this in the context of encouraging questions, debate and reflection so that 'learning by doing' was not just an activity but also a way to engage in some critical thinking. The motor vehicle apprentices did not just learn how to change a carburettor. They also developed their own questioning skills and ability to assess others, while the hairdressing students evaluated their own individual strengths and areas for further development.

Meeting in the middle

It is clear that in the outstanding lessons a selection of principles and techniques from both orientations had been combined into a compromise approach. There is a difference, though, in respect of the various segments of the lifelong learning sector identified in Chapter 1. The vocational lessons had much in common with behaviourist principles, although they all incorporated a significant number of features that would not be associated with this particular learning theory. They certainly included elements of a cognitivist and humanistic approach to teaching and learning. In contrast to this, the remedial, community and academic lessons were located more towards constructivism but they had as their starting points behaviourist learning outcomes.

If taken at face value, and given the earlier suggestion of behaviourism as 'bad' and constructivism as 'good', this might imply an age-old academic versus vocational divide and the assumption that abstract knowledge is worthier than practical knowledge. However, the sample includes different types of lessons and so judgements of outstanding have clearly taken into account the appropriateness of the teaching and assessment methods depending on the context. Considering the diversity of the sector and the complexities of teaching and learning it is unsurprising to find that there is no one approach or rigid template that works for all lessons.

Neither, though, do the lessons dovetail easily with the educational theories most frequently associated with notions of excellent practice. One way of reflecting this is to plot each lesson onto the kind of continua suggested by John Lea (2012: part 6). An 'ideal' lesson would be located to the right-hand side on every line. As can be seen in Figure 7.1, which is an amended version of Lea's model, although mostly on the right when plotted on these continua, the 20 outstanding lessons are not all neatly aligned to the 'correct' end. This is not a scientific method by any means but it provides a helpful visual representation of the lessons. It reflects the fact that the five vocational lessons veer towards behaviourism, as discussed above. While these lessons are also in a similar position in relation to training/education, the animal care, media studies and social work lessons fall broadly in the middle between these extremes. The continua also highlight the significant use of inductive teaching and learning, assessment *for* learning and the extent to which students took a deep approach to their learning. As is very clear, all the lessons were participatory rather than didactic.

Behaviourist   Constructivist

Didactic   Participatory

Deductive   Inductive

Assessment of learning   Assessment for learning

Surface learning   Deep learning

Training   Education

Behaviourist/constructivist reflects the discussion in this chapter, with the five vocational lessons more towards the left-hand side.

Didactic/participatory demonstrates that there was very little didactic teaching and students were participative in all the lessons.

Deductive/inductive reflects the extent to which teachers taught by telling as opposed to allowing students to discover what they were required to learn through tasks, discussions or questioning.

Assessment of/assessment for learning highlights the proportion of time in the lessons concentrating on assessing the learning the students had demonstrated, rather than promoting their further learning.

Surface/deep learning demonstrates the approach taken by the teacher to foster deep learning, through teaching and assessment.

Training/education reflects the emphasis taken by the teacher as to the purpose of the lesson. Training is taken to mean that the focus is on *how* to gain one or more specific skills. Education is much broader, addressing the development of students' knowledge and intellect, and accommodates, where appropriate, the *why* as well as the *how*.

Figure 7.1   Twenty lessons plotted on an adaptation of John Lea's continua

Chapter summary

Evidence from these 20 lessons suggests that there is no 'typical' outstanding lesson, in terms of subject, setting or level. The lessons included a variety of subjects in the vocational, academic, remedial and community segments of the lifelong learning sector, at varying levels and in different types of institution. They featured no specific resources and are not taught by any particular type of teacher, in terms of age or experience. There were no typical students. Students varied from school pupils to mature adults, representing a very wide range of backgrounds, attitudes and values.

The common features across the 20 lessons were the factors that teachers had responsibility for and could control. Therefore, it is the *teachers* who made the lessons outstanding. This may seem obvious but it is worth emphasizing their expert knowledge and high-level skills, in the context of an environment where the role of the teacher is increasingly downplayed, as discussed in Chapter 1. While they could not choose the setting or the students, the teachers did plan, select, apply, adapt and evaluate the teaching and assessment methods they used in these lessons. The teaching methods they chose were based on problem-solving and/or authentic tasks, discovery rather than telling, structured discussions and independent learning. Assessment was congruent with learning. It was valid, helpful to both students and teachers and aligned closely to the teaching approach.

8 Myths and evidence

The extent to which practice in these 20 lessons matches the models of outstanding teaching and learning held by teachers and managers in the lifelong learning sector is not known. Further research and a more open debate about pedagogy among the relevant agencies would be helpful in this respect.

Anecdotal information, supported by research (O'Leary 2012), as discussed in Chapter 1, suggests that it is not uncommon for teachers to adapt their teaching to what they perceive to be the prevalent inspection zeitgeist. This leads to interesting discussions, on occasion, whereby teachers are put in the position of defending a particular practice or the use of a resource because they believe that is what is expected of them, without having a sound educational rationale to support their choice. This was evident, for example, a few years after the creation in 2003 of the Standards Unit, which had been established to identify and disseminate good practice as part of the government's *Success for All* strategy (DfES 2002). The unit produced a variety of resources for several different curriculum areas. One such resource – packs of subject-specific 'playing cards' – was particularly popular and frequently used in lessons when observers were present. In a well-intentioned attempt to encourage active learning, the idea was that students, usually working in pairs or groups, selected a question card and matched it to the correct response or definition card. Creative though the resources were, they could not in themselves transform teaching and learning. As with any other resource or activity, what is important is the expertise of the teacher in deciding how to use it, if at all, to support or assess learning and how it could fit into the overall purpose and shape of the lesson. At worst, the card games were an adjunct to mediocre lessons simply because they had been deemed by someone else to be 'good practice'. At best, teachers used their professional judgement as to whether or not to use the material produced by the Standards Unit. Where they did, they integrated the card games and other resources into their well-planned and clearly structured lessons in an imaginative way.

It may be helpful at this point to dispel certain myths about practice, observation and inspection.

Ten myths

Contrary to the evidence in the form of these 20 lessons, there is a view, expressed by both teachers and managers in the lifelong learning sector that, particularly when being observed, teachers *must* do the following.

1 Read out learning outcomes at the start of every lesson

None of the teachers began their lessons by showing on a whiteboard or reading out aloud a list of learning outcomes. It is clearly sensible, and educationally sound, in most cases to set the lesson in the context of previous and future lessons, to inform students, in jargon-free language that they understand, what they will be learning, why and, if appropriate, how. However, sometimes teachers, applying their professional judgement, have good reason to use a different type of terminology, delay this information, change direction or to build in an element of surprise. Reading out outcomes at the start of a lesson is rarely associated with inspirational practice.

2 Present the perfect lesson plan

In an attempt to create the perfect lesson plan, with learning outcomes written in such a way that they can easily be assessed, there is a real danger that the focus is on *how* the lesson is taught in terms of teaching methods, and *how* the outcomes are met, at the expense of *what* is actually taught and *how* it is learned. The teachers of the outstanding lessons provided lesson plans of varying quality and quantity, often not reflecting fully the significant preparation they had clearly undertaken. Some attached extensive notes about students' backgrounds and prior attainment as well as individual targets and other information pertaining to progress. Others were more restrained. They all wrote relatively jargon-free learning outcomes but this did not mean that the outcomes themselves were simplistic. As emphasized throughout this book, a key feature of the outstanding lessons was the high expectations the teachers had of their students.

3 Put on a performance

It would be naive to suggest that the teachers did not prepare particularly well, knowing that they would be observed. However, if it were easy for teachers to put on a performance for a 'one-off' excellent lesson, there would be many more lessons graded outstanding. In the 20 outstanding lessons, it was very clear to the experienced observers that the teachers knew their students well, were building on work completed in previous lessons, had established relationships that had developed over time and had taken into consideration prior attainment that had been acquired gradually.

4 Always put students in pairs or groups

There was a clear rationale for the use of pair and group work in those outstanding lessons where this approach was adopted. In these lessons, students worked on meaningful tasks that were integral to the shape, flow and content of the lesson. However, pair and group activities are not an essential ingredient of an outstanding lesson. As has been shown, many of the outstanding lessons involved students working on their own, sitting at a computer or engaged in whole-class discussions. Pair and group work for the sake of it may well be inappropriate and no better than listening to a lecture for the same period of time. In fact, a well-constructed and interesting lecture would be a better option for the students. If directed to work in pairs or in a larger group on an irrelevant, boring or purposeless task, students will become disinterested and/or disruptive. They are also as likely to pool ignorance as they are to share expertise.

5 Keep changing activities

It is generally considered to be good practice to change activities and teaching methods in a lesson frequently, so as to maintain students' interest, meet their varying learning preferences and make lessons fun. There was some evidence to support this approach in the outstanding lessons but, as with the previous myth, this strategy is not essential and sometimes it is inappropriate. Too often the perceived need to keep changing activities drives the lesson and is not informed by decisions as to what to teach and how. Some of the outstanding lessons were quite traditional in format and style, reliant on one main teaching method, and others primarily involved students working mostly on their own. What they all have in common is that, whatever the approach, the teaching methods were closely aligned to the nature of the discipline, the learning outcomes and the assessment method(s).

6 Avoid student presentations when being observed

Some consider a lesson that involves student presentations to be not *real* teaching because the teacher is not seen *in action*. Two the 20 outstanding lessons fall into this category. Teachers may be reluctant to take the risk of using student presentations when an observer is present, fearing that the students will let them down in some way or that they, as teachers, may be perceived as getting away with not doing anything. While some might argue that a judgement on the lesson may be unfair because it will be based on the performance of the students, the counterargument is that this is precisely the reason why it *is* fair. In the two examples in this book, the work of the teacher in preparing students before the lesson was evident and the quality of the presentations and subsequent questions and debate gave a very clear indication as to the students' level of knowledge and skill.

7 Always use technology

Technology can be used creatively, innovatively and helpfully to support teaching and learning but it is not the case that, in order to be judged outstanding, a lesson *must* include some aspect of e-learning. Some of the outstanding lessons involved no technology, although it may have been a factor in the preparation or homework. Teachers used computers, interactive whiteboards and vocationally specific equipment and resources to support them and their students but these were not seen as a starting point on which to base the lesson. There was no evidence of the use of technology, or any other resources, for the sake of it or to meet the requirements of an observation checklist.

8 Use information on students' learning styles to plan lessons

In planning, lesson management and assessment, the teachers of outstanding lessons demonstrated that they knew their students well. They matched tasks and questions very carefully to students' knowledge and skill levels and, in some cases, to other issues associated with inclusion, social issues or personality. An extreme of this approach was evident in the one lesson where the teacher devised tailor-made tasks for each of her students. What the teachers did *not* do was to label students as types of learners, such as 'pragmatist' or 'left-brainer', on the basis of questionnaires they had completed once at the beginning of their course and then plan their lessons for the rest of the academic year around this information.

9 Always address equality and diversity explicitly

Some of the teachers of outstanding lessons planned ways to promote equality and diversity in their subject, while others very skilfully took advantage of naturally occurring opportunities to do so during the lessons. All the teachers created a highly inclusive environment, as discussed in Chapter 6 and their attitudes, language and behaviour suggested that they genuinely saw difference as a resource rather than as a problem. In some lessons, though, there may be no reason to address equality and diversity explicitly. If teachers believe they are required to do so in every lesson and particularly those in which they are being observed, it can lead to a token-istic, simplistic and cynical approach and will be counterproductive. This may be the unintended consequence of well-intentioned institutional poli-cies that are not supported by appropriate professional development.

10 Never deviate from the lesson plan

Detailed lesson plans with specific timings are very helpful, particularly for trainee and new teachers. Teachers need to use their judgement, though, on the odd occasion when it is clearly appropriate to deviate from the plan – for example, to take advantage of a turn of events externally or within the classroom or when the lesson is just not working. Almost all the teachers of the 20 outstanding lessons kept broadly to the content, activity and timings in their lessons plans. It is likely that many more teachers deviate from lesson plans when not being observed.

Five common features

Whether or not HMI were measuring what they should have been measur-ing remains open to ongoing debate, as discussed in Chapter 1. While the lessons may not conform to specific theoretical notions of 'excellence', as reflected in the previous chapter, this book has highlighted what, in prac-tice, these particular 20 lessons *did* have in common, whether they were vocational, remedial, community or academic.

Firstly, they were extremely well planned. This did not necessarily present itself in the form of meticulous lesson plans but it was evident that considerable thought had gone into the choice of teaching and assessment methods, as well as resources. Each aspect of the lesson was closely aligned to maximize opportunities, within the given time frame, for students to learn. Teachers planned carefully to ensure that all of their students would be actively involved in meaningful learning, at a sufficiently challenging level and that they would be given plenty of formative feedback to help them make sense of what they were learning and what they needed to do to make further progress.

Secondly, teachers were passionate and enthusiastic about both their subject and their teaching. They appeared to want genuinely to be in the lesson in order to share that passion and to help their students to learn, enjoy learning and achieve well. Thirdly, the teachers demonstrated con-siderable expertise in the way they asked questions. They did this to check levels of understanding, elicit information and views and encourage think-ing and discovery. Fourthly, these teachers demanded high standards and students responded readily by meeting those expectations. It was certainly not the case that these teachers had 'easy' students. Students' high levels of motivation were, to a large extent, a product of the way they were taught and the skilfully subtle manner in which teachers managed their lessons. Fifthly, and finally, teachers had established respectful and professional relationships with their students. The atmosphere they created was highly inclusive, with a focus on a serious approach to learning, while at the same time making learning enjoyable for all students, regardless of their background or prior attainment.

The considerable expertise of these teachers deserves to be acknowledged, celebrated and disseminated.

Glossary

In the text, the first mention of a glossary item appears in **bold**.

Active learning
Teaching and learning approaches that require students to be active – for example reading, writing, discussing or problem-solving, rather than simply listening or observing.

Advance organizer
Information presented by the teacher to help students to organize and interpret what comes next in the lesson.

Andragogy
Most widely associated with Malcolm Knowles, andragogy is what he described as the art and science of helping adults to learn.

Behaviourism/behaviourist approach
A philosophy of learning that focuses on objectively observable behaviours and defines learning as the acquisition of new behaviour.

Closed question
A question that can be answered with just one word or a short phrase.

Cognitivism/cognitive approach
A school of thought that places emphasis on students and how they gain and organize their knowledge.

Community of practice
A community made up of those who share common understandings and practices, who might extend or create knowledge by virtue of these shared practices.

Constructive alignment
Ensuring that teaching and assessment methods are well matched to learning outcomes.

Constructivism/constructivist approach
An approach suggesting that learning is the process of adjusting the rules and mental models students each generate to accommodate new

experiences and that by reflecting on these experiences they construct their own new meaning.

Convergent question
A question to which there is a single or accepted correct answer.

Declarative knowledge
Knowledge that can be 'declared', usually by telling people about it, orally or in writing.

Deductive
An approach to teaching and learning whereby the teacher provides information and/or explains concepts to students, often in the form of generalizations with examples and then students apply, test or practise what has been taught.

Deep approach to learning
An approach whereby students relate ideas to each other and actively seek to understand what they are being taught.

Didactic teaching
A teaching method based on transmission of information by the teacher with little, if any, active involvement by the students.

Discovery learning
A teaching approach that provides students with structured opportunities to discover information, facts, relationships and concepts for themselves, without being told directly; it is also known as guided discovery learning, inquiry-based or problem-based learning.

Divergent question
A question to which there are a number of possible answers, many of which may be acceptable.

Experiential learning
Learning that involves or relates to experience.

Formative assessment
Informal or formal feedback given to students, during or between lessons, that does not contribute to final grades but is used to identify how well they are doing and what they need to do to improve; it can also be used by teachers to judge their own effectiveness.

Functioning knowledge
Knowledge that can be applied, as in practical knowledge.

Higher order questions
Questions that invite students to explore an idea in depth and give an answer that is expansive.

Humanistic psychology
When applied to teaching, humanistic psychology emphasizes students' intrinsic motivation and the role of the teacher as a facilitator of learning.

Inclusive practice
Inclusive teaching refers to the creation of a learning environment that provides all students, regardless of their background, with the opportunity to fulfil their own learning potential, acknowledging that students learn in different ways and are members of diverse communities.

Inductive
An approach to teaching and learning whereby students are exposed to instances or examples, from which they recognize patterns and/or make their own generalization; the teacher's role is to create the opportunities for this to happen.

Learning outcomes
Statements in course or syllabus documentation and/or lesson plans that articulate what students will be able to do by the end of the course or lesson.

Lower order questions
Questions to students that require them to recall information or memorized facts.

Open question
A question that cannot be answered with one word and instead requires a long and/or well-considered response.

Outcomes-based education/system/method
Education based on the practice of measuring students' performance.

Pedagogy
The practice of teaching and the associated values, beliefs and theories that underpin this teaching.

Practical knowledge
Knowledge that can be applied.

Scaffolding
The assistance provided by teachers, usually by a phased introduction to progressively more difficult concepts or activities, to move students beyond their current level of knowledge and/or skills.

Socratic questioning
Skilful questioning that encourages students to explore, consider, reason and evidence, and project forward to reflect on consequences and implications.

Summative assessment
Feedback, usually written, to students on their work, leading to a final mark or descriptor; it is used to grade, select and predict future performance.

Surface approach to learning
An approach whereby students take a narrow view of learning and are most concerned with reproducing material for assessments, without a desire to understand what they have been taught.

Bibliography

Abbott, J. (1994) Learning Makes Sense: Re-creating education for a changing future, Letchworth: Education 2000, quoted in Effective Learning, *NSIN Research Matters*, 17, Summer 2002. London: Institute of Education, University of London.

Alexander, R. (2008) *Education for All, the Quality Imperative and the Problem of Pedagogy*. Create Pathways to Access, Research Monograph 20. London: Institute of Education, University of London.

Armitage, A., Bryant, R., Dunnill, R., Flanagan, K., Hayes, D., Hudson, A., Kent, J., Lawes, S. and Renwick, M. (2007) *Teaching and Training in Post-Compulsory Education*, 3rd edition. Maidenhead: Open University Press.

Ausubel, D. P. (1960) The Use of Advance Organizers in the Learning and Retention of Meaningful Verbal Material, *Journal of Educational Psychology*, 51(5): 267–72.

Avis, J. (2009) *Teaching in Lifelong Learning: A guide to theory and practice*. Maidenhead: Open University Press.

Bailey, B. and Robson, J. (2004) Learning Support Workers in Further Education in England: A hidden revolution?, *Journal of Further and Higher Education*, 28(4): 373–93.

Bandura, A. (1986) *Social Foundations of Thought and Action: A social cognitive theory*. Englewood Cliffs, NJ: Prentice-Hall.

Biggs, J. (1999) *Teaching for Quality Learning at University*. Buckingham: Society for Research into Higher Education and Open University Press.

Black, P. and William, D. (1998) *Inside the Black Box: Raising standards through classroom assessment*. London: School of Education, King's College.

Bloom, B. S. (ed.) (1956) *Taxonomy of Educational Objectives: The classification of educational goals*, Handbook I: *Cognitive Domain*. New York: David McKay.

Boud, D., Keogh, R. and Walker, D. (1985) *Reflection: Turning experience into learning*. London: Kogan Page.

Brown, G. and Wragg, E. C. (1993) *Questioning*. London: Routledge.

Brown, J. S., Collins, A. and Duguid, P. (1989) Situated Cognition and the Culture of Learning, *Educational Researcher*, 18(1): 32–42.

Brown, S. and Knight, P. (1994) *Assessing Learners in Higher Education*. London: Kogan Page.

Bruner, J. (1960) The Importance of Structure, in J. Bruner (ed.) *The Process of Education*. Cambridge, MA: Harvard University Press, 16–32.

Bruner, J. (1966) *Toward a Theory of Instruction*. Cambridge, MA: Harvard University Press.

Coffield, F. (2008) *Just Suppose Teaching and Learning Became the First Priority*. London: Learning and Skills Network.

Coffield, F. and Edward, S. (2009) Rolling out 'Good', 'Best' and 'Excellent' Practice. What next? Perfect practice?, *British Educational Research Journal*, 35(3): 371–90.

Coffield, F., Edward, S., Finlay, I., Hodgson, A., Spours, K. and Steer, R. (2008) *Improving Learning, Skills and Inclusion: The impact of policy on post-compulsory education*. Abingdon: Routledge.

Coffield, F., Moseley, D., Hall, E. and Ecclestone, K. (2004a) *Learning Styles and Pedagogy in Post-16 Learning: A systematic and critical review*. London: Learning and Skills Research Centre, Learning and Skills Development Agency.

Coffield, F., Moseley, D., Hall, E. and Ecclestone, K. (2004b) *Should We be Using Learning Styles?: What research has to say in practice*. London: Learning and Skills Research Centre, Learning and Skills Development Agency.

Cox, A. and Harper, H. (2001) *Planning Teaching and Assessing Learning*. Greenwich, CT: Greenwich University Press.

Curzon, L. B. (ed.) *Teaching in Further Education*, 4th edition. London: Cassell.

Day, C. (2009) A Passion for Quality: Teachers who make a difference, *Tijdschrift voor Lerarenopleiders*, 30(3): 4–13.

Department for Education and Skills (DfES) (2002) *Success For All: Reforming further education and training: Our vision for the future*. London: DfES.

Dewey, J. (1916) *Democracy and Education*. New York: Macmillan.

Dillon, J. T. (1988) *Questioning and Teaching: A manual of practice*. London: Croom Helm.

Dillon, J. T. (1994) *Using Discussion in Classrooms*. Buckingham: Open University Press.

Ecclestone, K. and Hayes, D. (2009) *The Dangerous Rise of Therapeutic Education*. New York: Routledge.

Eraut, M. (2004) Transfer of Knowledge Between Education and Workplace Settings, in H. Rainbird, A. Fuller and A. Munro (eds) *Workplace Learning in Context*. London: Routledge, 201–21.

Farrell, T. (2002) Lesson Planning, in J. C. Richards and W. A. Renandya (eds) *Methodology in Language Teaching: An anthology of current practice*. Cambridge: Cambridge University Press, 30–40.

Feather, N. (ed.) (1982) *Expectations and Actions*. Hillsdale, NJ: Erlbaum.

Fried, R. L. (1995) *The Passionate Teacher*. Boston, MA: Beacon Press.

Fry, H., Ketteridge, S. and Marshall, S. (eds) (2009) *A Handbook for Teaching and Learning in Higher Education: Enhancing academic practice*, 3rd edition. Abingdon: Routledge.

Fuller, A. and Unwin, L. (2003) Learning as Apprentices in the Contemporary UK Workplace: Creating and managing expansive and restrictive participation, *Journal of Education and Work*, 16(4): 406–27.

Furedi, F. (2012) The Unhappiness Principle, *Times Higher Educational Supplement*, 29 November 2012.

Gagné, R. M. (1970) *The Conditions of Learning*. New York: Holt, Rinehart & Winston.

Gibbs, G. (1988) *Learning by Doing: A guide to teaching and learning methods*. London: Further Education Unit.

Gibbs, G. (2012) *Implications of 'Dimensions of Quality' in a Market Environment*. York: Higher Education Academy.

Gibbs, G. and Habeshaw, T. (2002) *Recognising and Rewarding Excellent Teachers*. Milton Keynes: Open University Press and National Co-ordination Team for the Teaching Quality Enhancement Fund.

Glasner, A. (2003) Can All Teachers Aspire to Excellence?, *Exchange*, 5: 11.

Harper, H. (1997) *Management in Further Education: Theory and practice*. London: David Fulton.

Hillier, Y. (2005) *Reflective Teaching in Further and Adult Education*. London: Continuum.

Huxley, M. (2001) Mismatch and Disruption, in C. Atkinson, and B. Chandler (eds) *Student Support: Tutoring, guidance and dealing with disruption*. Greenwich, CT: Greenwich University Press, 157–160.

John, P. (2006) Lesson Planning and the Student Teacher: Re-thinking the dominant model, *Journal of Curriculum Studies*, 38(4): 483–98.

Knight, P. and Yorke, M. (2003) *Assessment, Learning and Employability*. Maidenhead: Society for Research into Higher Education and Open University Press.

Knowles, M. S. (1980) *The Modern Practice of Adult Education: From pedagogy to andragogy*. Englewood Cliffs, NJ: Cambridge Adult Education.

Kohler, W. (1925) *The Mentality of Apes*. New York: Harcourt Brace Jovanovitch.

Kounin, J. S. (1977) *Discipline and Group Management in Classrooms*. Huntington, NY: R. E. Krieger.

Lave, J. and Wenger, E. (1991) *Situated Learning: Legitimate peripheral participation*. Cambridge: Cambridge University Press.

Lea, J. (2012) *77 Things to Think About . . . Teaching and Learning in Higher Education*. Canterbury: Canterbury Christ Church University.

Lingfield, R. (2012) *Professionalism in Further Education: Final report of the Independent Review Panel*. London: Department of Business, Innovation and Skills.

Little, B., Locke, W., Parker, J. and Richardson, J. (2007) *Excellence in Teaching and Learning: A review of the literature for the Higher Education Academy*. Milton Keynes: Centre for Higher Education Research and Information at the Open University.

Luckin, R., Bligh, B., Manches, A., Ainsworth, S., Crook, C. and Noss, R. (2012) *Decoding Learning: The proof, promise and potential of digital learning*. London: Nesta.

McGregor, D. (1966) *Leadership and Motivation*. Cambridge, MA: MIT Press.

Martinez, P. (2001) *Great Expectations: Setting targets for students*. London: Learning and Skills Development Agency.

Marton, F. and Säljö, R. (1976) On Qualitative Differences in Learning: 1 – Outcome and Process, *British Journal of Educational Psychology*, 46(1): 4–11.

Minton, D. (1991) *Teaching Skills in Further and Adult Education*. Basingstoke: Macmillan.

Morgan, N. and Saxton, J. (1991) *Teaching, Questioning and Learning*. London: Routledge.

Office for Standards in Education (Ofsted) (2003) *The Initial Training of Further Education Teachers – A Survey*. London: Ofsted. Available at: www.ofsted.gov.uk (accessed May 2013).

Office for Standards in Education (Ofsted) (2012a) *The Annual Report of Her Majesty's Chief Inspector of Education, Children's Services and Skills 2011/12*. London: Ofsted. Available at: www.ofsted.gov.uk (accessed May 2013).

Office for Standards in Education (Ofsted) (2012b) *The Initial Training of Further Education and Skills Teachers – A Survey*. London: Ofsted. Available at: www.ofsted.gov.uk (accessed May 2013).

O'Leary, M. (2012) Time to Turn Worthless Lesson Observation into a Powerful Tool for Teaching and Learning, *InTuition/CPD Matters* (Institute for Learning), 9: 16–18.

Pavlov, I. P. (1927) *Conditioned Reflexes*. Mineola, NY: Courier Dover Publications.

Petty, G. (2006) *Evidence-Based Teaching: A practical approach*. Cheltenham: Nelson Thornes.

Race, P. (2005) *Making Learning Happen*. London: Sage Publications.

Race, P., Brown, S. and Smith, B. (2005) *500 Tips on Assessment*, 2nd edition, London: Routledge.

Race, P. and Pickford, R. (2007) *Making Teaching Work: 'Teaching smarter' in post-compulsory education*. London: Sage Publications.

Ramsden, P. (2003) *Learning to Teach in Higher Education*, 2nd edition. Abingdon: Routledge.

Reece, I. and Walker, S. (2007) *Teaching, Training and Learning: A practical guide*, 6th edition revised, ed. D. Clues and M. Charlton. Sunderland: Business Education Publishers.

Rogers, C. (1983) *Freedom to Learn for the '80s*. Columbus, OH: Merrill.

Rowntree, D. (1987) *Assessing Students: How shall we know them?* London: Kogan Page.

Schön, D. A. (1982) *The Reflective Practitioner: How professionals think in action*. New York: HarperCollins.

Skinner, B. F. (1974) *About Behaviourism*. New York: Random House.

Smith, C. and Laslett, R. (2001) Four Rules of Classroom Management, in C. Atkinson and B. Chandler (eds) *Student Support: Tutoring, guidance and dealing with disruption*. Greenwich, CT: Greenwich University Press, 149–156.

Tavistock Institute (2002) *Review of Current Pedagogic Research and Practice in the Fields of Post-Compulsory Education and Lifelong Learning*. Exeter: Economic and Social Research Council Teaching and Learning Research Programme.

Tedder, M. and Lawy, R. (2010) 'Passionate about Teaching' – the Role of Mentors in Implementing Professional Standards, *Teaching in Lifelong Learning: A Journal to Inform and Improve Practice*, 2(2): 45–55.

Thomas, L. and May, H. (2010) *Inclusive Learning and Teaching in Higher Education*. York: Higher Education Academy.

Tyler, R. W. (1949) *Basic Principles of Curriculum and Instruction*. Chicago, IL: University of Chicago Press.

Vygotsky, L. S. (1962) *Thought and Language*. Cambridge, MA: MIT Press.

Vygotsky, L. S. (1978) *Mind in Society: The development of higher psychological processes*. Cambridge, MA: Harvard University Press.

Watson, J. (1928) *The Ways of Behaviourism*. New York: Harper & Brothers.

Wolf, A. (1993) *Assessment Issues and Problems in a Criterion-Based System*. London: Further Education Unit.

Wood, K. (2011) *Education: The basics*. Abingdon: Routledge.

Wragg, E. C. (1999) *An Introduction to Classroom Observation*, 2nd edition. London: Routledge.

Wright, A.-M., Abdi-Jama, S., Colquhoun, S., Speare, J. and Partridge, T. (2006) *FE Lecturer's Guide to Diversity and Inclusion*. London: Continuum.

Index

POWERFUL TECHNIQUES FOR TEACHING IN LIFELONG LEARNING

Stephen D. Brookfield

9780335244775 (Paperback)
2013

eBook also available

Powerful Techniques for Teaching in Lifelong Learning is a practical handbook that offers a range of helpful ideas and approaches for working with older learners. Written in an accessible and conversational style, it draws on the author's vast experience of working with older learners and tackles some of the major challenges and problems you are likely to face in teaching older learners, such as addressing inequality and diversity and dealing with resistance.

Key features:

- Teaching for critical thinking
- Using discussion
- Self-directed learning

www.openup.co.uk

CREATIVE TEACHING APPROACHES IN THE LIFELONG LEARNING SECTOR

Brendon Harvey and Josie Harvey

9780335246304 (Paperback)
December 2012

eBook also available

This practical book explores creative ways of teaching and learning in the lifelong learning sector and provides a toolkit of creative teaching approaches with the potential to transform your teaching practice.

Drawing on various techniques and diverse environments the book illustrates a variety of approaches, offering insights and conclusions drawn from a rich range of practice examples and highlighting the potential pitfalls of creative practices.

Key features:

- Draws on a variety of techniques and environments to illustrate aspects of creative approaches for LLS
- Reflective prompts throughout each chapter to encourage the reader to look at emerging practice and engage with creative approaches

www.openup.co.uk

ENHANCING LEARNING THROUGH TECHNOLOGY IN LIFELONG LEARNING
Fresh Ideas: Innovative Strategies

Steve Ingle and Vicky Duckworth

9780335246403(Paperback)
March 2013

eBook also available

This book provides an essential resource for both new and experienced teachers, trainers and lecturers looking to harness the benefits of technology in their approaches to teaching, learning and assessment. Those working across the Lifelong Learning Sector, including schools and universities, face increasing pressures in demonstrating their purposeful engagement with technology to provide outstanding teaching and learning, and professional standards place a clear emphasis on the demonstrable use of emerging technology.

Key features:

- Each example demonstrates how a range of online, Web 2.0 and other technologies can be used to create engaging, interactive and learner centric lessons which promote retention and achievement.
- Example technologies include micro-blogging, the use of avatars and virtual worlds, simple recording devices and the interactive features of common office applications.
- Whatever their level of technical ability, teaching practitioners and those supporting learning will find new ideas to enhance their approaches to creative teaching and learning with the use of technology

www.openup.co.uk

OPEN UNIVERSITY PRESS
McGraw - Hill Education